Option Trading

Advanced Guide for Beginners that Shows you All the Day and Swing Strategies Simplified To Make Big Money in 2020 investing in Stocks, Futures, ETF Market and Binaries RIGHT NOW

Table of Contents

Introduction

If you were to find an investor and ask to look at their portfolio, you will be able to see that they have a large variety of investments that they are working on. They don't just put all their money on one company all the time. Instead they have many different types of investments they can work with such as bonds, stocks, mutual funds, and more. In addition, there are times when a portfolio will include options, but it is not as likely to be there as some of the others.

This is like getting a key where once you use that key to open the front door of a house, then it belongs to you. You may not technically own the house because you have the key, but you can use that key whenever you would like and if you choose, you could purchase the house later on.

Options are set up so that they cost you a certain fixed price for so much time. This length will change based on the option that you are working with. Sometimes you will have an option that only lasts for a day and then there are some that you may hold onto for a few years. You will know how long the option is going to last before you make the purchase.

Options are nothing new. It's a well-known term in trading, and even though it might be overwhelming for some people to think about, options are not really hard to understand. The portfolios of investors are generally composed of different classes of assets, which can be bonds, mutual funds, stocks or even ETFs. One such asset class are options, and certain advantages are offered by them when used accurately, which other trading stocks and ETFs cannot offer. Like many other asset classes, options too can be purchased with brokerage investment accounts.

Options can be considered as an investment that gives you more "options."

But that does not mean that there are no risks involved. Almost every investment entails a multitude of risks. The same goes for options. An investor ought to know of these risks before proceeding with trade.

Options are a part of the group of securities called derivatives. The term derivative is many a time associated with huge risks and volatile performance. Warren Buffett once called derivatives "weapons of mass destruction," which is a little too much.

Options are a kind of derivative. Investors are often talking about different derivatives. Options derive their value from an underlying stock or security. In fact, options belong to the class of securities known as derivatives. For a long time, people associated derivatives with high-risk investments. This notion is not really true.

Derivatives obtain their value from an underlying security. Think about wine, for instance. Wine is produced from grapes. We also have ketchup which is derived from tomatoes. This is basically how derivatives function.

One can gain a real advantage in the market if they know how options work and can use them properly since you can put the cards in your favor if you can use options correctly. The great thing about options is that you can use them according to your style. If you're a speculative person, earn through speculation. If not, earn without speculating. You should know how options work even if you decide never to use them because other companies you invest in might use options.

Options are an attractive investment tool. They have a risk/reward framework, which is unlike any other. They can be used in a multitude of combinations that make them very versatile. The risk factor involved can be diluted by using these options with other financial instruments or other option contracts, and at the same time opening more avenues for profits. While many investments have an unbound quantum of risk attached, options' trading, on the other hand, has defined risks, which the buyers know about.

Chapter 1. What Is An Option?

An option is an agreement that enables you to purchase and sell specific stock trading amounts at a particular price within a particular trading time before the date of expiration avails. Options exist in two kinds: call options and put options. We are going to dive into the deep content of the mentioned kinds later on in the book.

The Best Options Trading Platform

There exist different trading platforms for options trading. Picking out a particular trading platform is not so easy. The selected trading site should first correspond to what you want to major on and its efficiency. Let us explore some of the best platforms for options trading with different features, and I hope that you spot the one that fascinates you:

TD Ameritrade: It has been ranked the best trading platform recently due to its reasonable pricing, excellent beginner sources, and top-notch platform suitable for professional options traders and experts. This kind of platform has something good for everyone, as depicted by its best options. Trading with TD Ameritrade is so worth it as depicted by its great platform, good learning materials, in-depth research, and better customer support. Below are some of the reasons why most traders venture into this kind of platform:

• Creative platforms - It is much detailed and this eventually makes the trader much informed, which is a great opportunity to the beginners and the experienced options traders.

• Extensive product access

• Adequate guidance

• 24/7 support

• No hidden fees

• Easy to use because it is pretty much simplified and therefore used by a good number of beginners

Trade Station: Experts are highly recommended to engage in this particular kind of platform as it costs $5 in each trade and $0.50 in each contract.

Charles Schwab Platform: This kind of platform mainly targets the novice in options trading. It provides a great experience and awesome customer service as evidenced by the in-depth research with great educational materials. Unique order types are believed to be highly involved.

Ally Invest: When the need to minimize options trading costs is so high, the Ally Invest trading platform becomes a favorable option. A low kind of investment can be considered when commencing trading without worrying about the issues of big minimum balances. This platform is commonly known for cheap trades, rock bottom rates, availability of easy entry points, and stellar ratings. Moreover, Ally Invests has no minimum amount required in their accounts.

Robinhood: This is a great platform for beginners to start from because limited risks are involved. Since there is no trading fee, options can be purchased and sold with the exception of interfering with the initial investment. Robinhood does not provide much of learning sources and research tools information, but if you are sure to get some good books, this trading platform is going to be much friendly.

Robinhood is loved as a good options trading platform because it is pretty much user-friendly and there are no commission fees involved.

Interactive Brokers: This platform is suitable for active traders who are likely to get involved in frequent small trades and not really for passive traders with just a few trades per year. This site is rated the best in providing the best commission rates.

Lightspeed Trader: This platform focuses on the active and experienced traders as it offers professional-grade trading platforms. There is low pricing for large-volume traders, and the right site for various brokerage needs to be involved during options.

E*Trade: It supports both novice and experts involved in options trading. This platform is well-detailed and contains quite a large amount of data and research tools that aid in building advanced options trading chains and trading ladders. It is common to the active kind of traders because of various reasons such as no commission fees, and the site is pretty much detailed, hence making the traders quite informed and their low minimum account balance value.

Gatsby: This platform is known to be best for retail investors, traders that are new to options, social traders, and millennial traders involved in options trading. It is adequately detailed with options trading information enough to give a particular novice trader the courage and skills to commence options trading without being such a mess.

Fidelity: In this platform, traders are guided in the right direction, and resources needed along the way are also provided. Large chunks of research tools and learning resources are available for education and guidance to ease the options trading process for the option of novice traders. Moreover, the fidelity platform offers phone support throughout in case of any complications experienced by any options trader. Fidelity platform is famous for great research and the necessary tools needed in options trading. It has a high functioning site and very good at research. However, not all tools present to this site are available to all the users.

Vanguard: This platform is best for investors who are planning to retire with the intention of long-term options trading and high volume earnings.

AvaTrade: This is an online site offering its customers with various contracts that they would initiate options trading between various buyers and sellers. This site is legit and reliable and it has been fully approved by the government and even termed as a good trading policy. It targets all kinds of traders such as the novice, experienced, intermediate, and many more.

Options Trading Vs. Stock Trading

There is a big difference between options trading and stock trading.

Stock represents partial ownership of the company implying that when you purchase a stock, you are normally a part of the company. On the other hand, options trading is merely any ownership of a certain company; it is a contract involving a trader and another party that allows the trader to purchase or sell a certain amount of stock at a particular price within a specific period. The market may be so volatile but the strike prices reads are so high, and when the market activities are depicted to be calm, the strike prices may eventually be so down.

Let us look at some of the major differences between options trading and stock trading:

1.   Options tend to expire as depicted by the availability of expiration dates, while, on the other hand, stocks are much durable since they are properties of the company and bear no expiration dates. Therefore, stock trading is likely to happen for a longer period as compared to stock trading.

2.   Options derive the actual value from the value of the other assets involved during options trading, whereas stocks have a definite actual value that is fully recognized by the company in question.

3.   In the options trading activities, traders just have the full rights of the value amount. On the other hand, stock trading gives the traders gain full ownership of the property involved during trading activities.

4.   In options trading, the market predictability does not necessarily depend on the rates of supply and demand levels as compared to stock trading. With this in mind, the options trader is unlikely to predict what is happens to the market but he/she can, however, check on the volatility of the market.

5.   Options are much cheaper than stock. Money is so fundamental in trading and is always the biggest motivation in any kind of trading activity. Options are less expensive since the trader gets to acquire 100 shares of the equity during trading. Moreover, the cost of grasping an option contract is much cheaper as compared to purchasing and the underlying stock, and the trader acquires more amounts of benefits as compared to stock trading.

6.   Options are normally a great leverage tool in maximizing the amounts of profits gained during a particular trading period as compared to stock trading. This is evident in the collection of various amounts of premiums during the issuance of contracts hence increasing the amounts of profits collected in options trading as compared to stock trading.

7.   Options trading is much good at flexibility as compared to stock trading as evident in its tactical operations that happen frequently in various trading activities. Traders can make smaller investments that lead to good amounts of profits and fewer risks involved during a particular period. On the other hand, stock trading calls for good investments with multiple amounts of risks over an unspecified period.

8.   Another point is that options have a great chance of limiting the risks that are likely to be involved during trading, as compared to stock trading, where risk is pretty much unlimited during the unspecified period of trading.

9.   Options trading can better for you if your timing is okay, and as an options trader, you will be able to acquire larger amounts of profits during the contract as compared to when you would be involved in options trading.

10.   Options trading allows a particular option trader to bet where the market will not go–an activity that is not allowed in stock trading. The advantage of this opportunity is that there are higher chances of success than betting on where the market will go.

Terminologies Used in Options Trading

Option - It is a contract that allows an investor to purchase and sell a specific trading stock at a particular price within a particular period.

Call option - This is an equity agreement that awards a buyer the chance to purchase 100 particular shares at a particular strike price within a specified time. A seller is also needed to sell off the stock at a particular price if the option gets exercised.

Equity option - It is a kind of option that gives the owner, who happens to be the buyer, the chance to purchase and sell any available stock in the trading market at a specific share during a particular period before the expiration date is reached.

Commission - This is the fee charged in an options trading market after option orders have been executed on a securities exchange.

Strike price - This is the actual amount of price in which you choose to sell or buy options when you decide to exercise an option in the market.

Expiry date - This is the actual date–day, month, or year–to which a particular options trading contract becomes invalid and null.

Premium - It describes the price of an option, particularly the entire dollar value of the contract during a certain trading period.

Time decay - This is the erosion period when the value of time of a specific option diminishes as the expiration date reaches.

Put option - The kind of option where a buyer is given the privilege to sell 100 shares at a constant price before the expiration date. On another hand, the seller of a put option is required to purchase stock at a particular price if the trading option gets exercised at all.

Volume -This is the number of contracts that have been traded during a particular options trading period.

Holder - The specific owner of the contract is referred to as the holder in options trading.

Long Option - This simply implies having purchased an option at online transactions and therefore own it.

Short Option - This means to have sold the option in an opening transaction.

Change - The percentage term price of the last hour's sale in the options market.

Front-month - When the expiration of two months is involved in options trading, the month nearer in time is normally considered.

Index option - This is an option contract where the index is the underlying stock and not shares of any specific stock.

Time value - It describes the value to which time is attributable in options before a particular expiration date is reached.

Volatility - This is the actual fluctuation of prices of stocks in options trading where the stock prices keep rising and falling within time hence making it hard for traders to predict on future likely activities.

Contract - This is an agreement set between a buyer trader and a seller trader during a particular options trading activity.

Underlying asset - This is the 100 shares of stock that are involved in a particular agreement during a specified time.

Ask price - This is the lowest price that is being advertised in the options trading that anyone is willing to accept when selling a particular option at a particular period.

Last sale - It is the latest price that a certain option trader has traded within options trading.

Open interest - This is the number of the option that has been sold and also the ones that have not been brought back or in any case, exercise.

Bullish - This term is particularly referring to an investor who believes that a specific stock price will go higher or simply the market will rise higher.

Bearish - This term, on the other hand, describes a trader who believes that the market prices will do lower or the market will experience a downfall at a particular trading activity in a specific period.

Break-even point - This is the specific price that an underlying asset must reach to avoid the option buyer from acquiring losses if at all they decided to exercise the option.

Premium - This is the amount of income received by an option trader as he or she writes a contract off to another party.

Downside risk - This is the estimation of a particular downfall market price that is likely to be experienced by the market during the end of a particular trading period.

Implied volatility - This is an estimation of the future likelihood market volatility by analyzing the market status through the current activities occurring at the options trading market. Some traders get to use this as one of their strategies the options trading market to acquire large chunks of profits.

Index option - This is a kind of an option contract whose underlying security is an index and not shares of any specific stock.

Writing an option - This is to sell a call or put option contract that has been not possessed by any other trader in the market.

Mean - This is a mathematical operation where the total sum of observations in the market is divided by the particular number of observations in the market. The mean is used to provide data on various market values and the market standard deviation.

Spread - This is an option position established when a purchase of one option is established and a sale of an option too using the same underlying asset available in the trading market.

Historical volatility -This is analyzing the actual volatility of the past market occurrences and making the necessary helpful strategies and learning in your trading plan.

Credit - It is any value amount received in a particular trading account from the financial benefits experienced in various options trading activities. The profits and multiple benefits feed the trading accounts.

Debit - This is any amount of cash paid out to purchase an option during a particular trading period.

Horizontal - This is a term describing the options of the same strike price experienced in different months.

At the money - This term is used to describe the nearest price to the equity price during a particular trading moment.

Vertical - It is a term describing the options of different strike prices experienced in a particular month.

Resistance - This is a particular level where the equity price can not beyond any way higher, meaning that that particular price is the actual price limit.

Big chicken trade - This is a term used to describe a series of bull call calendars and the bear put calendars.

Ex-dividend - This is the actual date in which the stock enters the options trading market with the absence of dividends.

Selling to open - This ideally describes the selling of a particular option to open a position.

Selling to close - Selling a close means selling a specific option with the desire to close a particular position during options trading.

In the money - All the strike prices possess some intrinsic value where for a call, all strike prices are below the equity price whereas, for a put, all prices are the ones above the price of the equity.

Bid spread- This is the actual difference between the asking price and the bid price for a given option during a particular options trading period.

Dip in the money - This is a term used to refer to multiple in-the-money occurrences that have been experienced in a particular trading period in the options market.

Option spread - It is established by buying and selling equal amounts of options of a similar class with the same underlying security. However, the strike prices and expiration dates of the options are different.

Stock - It is described as a portion of a particular company belonging or ownership.

Margin - This is a particular amount of loan offered by a particular broker of a specific trader during a particular trading period.

Trading platform - This is a general trading site that traders interact with while making trading moves, buying, selling, and any other trading activities. Trading platforms consist of various kinds according to different variety of interests, and a trader gets to pick on a site in which he or she is most comfortable with.

Chapter 2. What Is Swing Trading?

Swing trading sounds suspicious, but as we'll see it's a solid middle-road type of investing in the stock market that will appeal to many people. Before we get into the specifics of what swing trading is, let's quickly discuss its evil twin, day trading. How does that work? Very briefly, day trading is a strategy that hopes to take advantage of a single day gain or loss. Some people see it as a "fast money" or "get rich quick" approach to stock market trading, but it's nothing of the sort. In order to engage in day trading, you must have an account with a minimum of $25,000 with a broker. So, if you're looking to make money on the stock market, but are short on cash, day trading isn't going to be something you can use to get rich.

Besides having a specific capital requirement, day trading requires active participation in the stock market that involves getting deeply invested in following financial news from many sources, trying to stay on top of rumors and breaking news, and watching every little move of your stocks throughout the day. You must do your due diligence with day trading. It also involves having some highly technical skills that most people who invest in the stock market would rather not bother with. The bottom line is that day trading is serious, and high-risk business. For our purposes, the key takeaway is that day trading attempts to leverage stock market gains (or losses, if you are shorting a stock) that occur within a single trading day. At the close, you're out of all your positions. This can be an advantage in that you avoid overnight risks, stocks can often take hits with trading on Asian and European markets.

We all know what long-term investing is. Basically, people try to set up a diverse portfolio of stocks (and other securities like bonds, mutual funds, etc.) in order to build long-term wealth. The definition of long-term might vary from person to person, it might be five years, ten years, or even three decades. Most people are probably thinking of building up some wealth over the course of their adult working years, so we are probably talking about a 25-30-year time window in most cases. Long-term investors may not even actively manage a portfolio, they might let a professional take care of that for them. If they do manage their own portfolio, they are going to invest using techniques like dollar cost averaging that minimize risks and take advantage of the average, longer-term behavior of the stock market. Over time, the trend of the stock market is up – and that is what people are after so they can build a 'nest egg'.

Some of us are more impatient, and, like the active involvement in the markets that day trading can provide. We love pouring over charts and graphs, studying companies and stock movements. Is there some kind of middle ground for these kinds of folks, who aren't up for day trading?

It turns out there is – and it's swing trading that we are after. Swing trading simply involves holding stocks for multiple days. One of the goals of swing trading is to give your investments some room for growth. With day trading, you're taking advantage of short-term gaps that increase the value of a stock. In swing trading, you're taking advantage of multi-day gaps up, so that you can build more gains from your investments. People think that day traders are the people who get rich on the stock market – and some do – but it's often swing traders who will make more money over the course of a year.

Since you're holding your investments for a bit longer, swing trading cuts down some of that risk that day traders have of making bad bets and incurring streaks of losses. So how long to swing traders hold their stocks?

It can vary quite a bit. Sometimes a swing trader will only hold a stock for a day or maybe two. But some swing traders hold stocks for 10 days, a month, 50 days, two months, or even out to 100 days (the definitions vary among swing traders – most would probably say 2 days up to a few weeks). You may completely hold onto a position, or you may sell a small part like 15% after 5 days and hold the rest for 30 days. There are more possibilities with swing trading.

Since you're holding your securities for a longer time period, you're exposing yourself to some risks that day traders aren't exposed to. For example, there can be short-term, dramatic events that can significantly influence stock prices over the course of a month or two. These could include war, terrorist attack, or even simply remarks from the President or The Fed. Swing traders are also more exposed to bad company news. Maybe the CEO gets arrested for corruption, or perhaps the company's product results in the deaths of some children. Swing traders, unlike day traders, hold their investments overnight, and so can be at a disadvantage when there are bad results in off-hours trading. These kinds of events are bad for all investors, but swing traders are more likely to take a negative hit from them than day traders. And long-term investors too – if you're holding stocks (and probably funds like the S&P 500) for anywhere from 5-30 years, those sorts of events often amount to background noise. Not so for the swing trader.

That said, in most cases swing trading provides a solid middle ground in between day trading and long-term investing that can help you grow wealth fast. Swing trading is also a bit slower paced than day trading. Many people view day trading as demanding, and that's a realistic perception. Swing trading is an alternative that lets people who like getting into the nitty-gritty of the markets but don't want the high pressure.

Of course, there are no guarantees in life, but let's start looking at the strategies employed by swing traders to help them earn profits.

How much capital do you need for swing trading

Unlike day trading, where brokers require you to have a minimum of $25,000 (and $30,000 is recommended) there aren't formal requirements for swing trading. Brokers pay special attention to day traders (and regulators do as well) but not so much for swing traders. That said, you will have to evaluate how much money you need to invest in order to reach your goals. But you can start small to get started if you like and remember that options trading lets you leverage a lot more power over the markets with smaller investments, so trading options is one way you can reduce your initial capital requirements.

However, a general rule of thumb according to market experts is that you should have around $10,000 in your account if you are a swing trader. Moreover, you should only risk 1% in a single trade, which for $10,000 would be $100. If you are more of a risk taker, you could risk up to 2%. You can manage your risk using stop-loss orders, which we will talk about below. The risk of a security losing value is called downside risk.

When it comes to minimum capital requirements, the following rules apply:

• A day trader is someone who makes more than 4 trades a week that open and closes on the same day.

- A day trader must have $25,000 in their account.

- There are no minimum requirements for swing trader accounts.

- However, if you cross that line of more than 4 trades a week that open and close on the same day, you'll be labeled a day trader and be forced to follow the rules for day traders.

- Swing traders have 2x leverage. So, if you invest $10,000, you can buy $20,000 worth of stock. Use leverage carefully, however. If you lose on your trades, you can end up owing more than what's in the account.

- When you're trading, you need to worry about commissions, not just the loss or gain on the stock. You should risk at least $100 on a trade to deal with commissions. Otherwise, they will eat up your profits or magnify your losses.

The way risk works

It's important to understand how traders evaluate risk. Some readers may misunderstand, thinking that when we say that you can risk $100 if you have a $10,000 account, that means you take your $100 and try to find a share or a few shares to buy. That isn't how it works.

First, you put in a stop-loss order. This is an order that you place after buying a stock that puts in an automatic sell order on your behalf if the stock price drops below a specific level. If we buy 10 shares of XYZ stock for $100 each, which will cost in total $1,000 (ignoring commissions, for the sake of simplicity), say we will place a stop-loss order of $90. This means that if the XYZ stock drops to $90 a share, our shares are automatically sold and we lost $10 a share, for a total loss of $100. If the stock is rapidly dropping, maybe it dropped to $85 a share. So, a stop-loss order is a type of insurance in the stock market, that prevents you from losing your shirt. It's also helpful for people who can't be in front of the computer all day long managing their investments – that way you have some automatic protection built in if things go south while you're not there. If you didn't place a stop-loss order and for some reason XYZ really tanked, you could end up losing a huge amount of money.

So, we see that the actual risk that we're talking about is going to be determined by looking at the price per share minus the amount we specify on the stop-loss order. Let's summarize:

• If a share is going for $200, and you place a stop-loss order of $180, the trade risk is $20.

• That means the amount you are willing to risk on a trade of 10 shares is $20 x 10 = $200. This is the account risk.

• If you have a $10,000 trading account, then your risk is 2%, since 0.02 x $10,000 = $200.

How much you risk is up to you, but these types of conservative figures are given because it's entirely possible that you're going to make multiple bad trades all right in a row. Of course, we're giving examples that aren't going to fit every situation. You can also minimize risk to different levels. In fact, more active traders put more stringent limits on risk than long-term investors do. The reason why is the following.

A stop-loss order has a risk of its own. Throughout the day, stock prices fluctuate a lot, and it has a random pattern over the short term that looks chaotic. So even if a stock is set to increase in value over the case of a day or a couple of days, over shorter time periods it may have some downturns in price. The risk is that one of these random fluctuations could drop the price at or below the limit you specify on the stop-loss order, and your shares will be sold. But then the stock climbs right back up. Day traders are concerned with fluctuations of the stock over the short term, so put tighter limits. As a swing trader, you might be planning on holding the stock for some time, but a lot less than a year. There could be longer-term trends that might trigger a stop-loss even though you're planning on holding the stock.

To see how this works, let's suppose that you bought some shares of Apple on 12/18/18, at $166.07 per share. We could put a stop-loss order on that of 5% to minimize our risk. Since 5% of $166.07 is $8.30, our stop-loss order will go in effect if the price drops below $157.77. That happened on December 20, when it dropped to $156.83. Our shares would have been sold. The stock bounced around a little and even dropped to $142 after New Year's so we might have felt good about ourselves at that point. However, by 3/21/19, the stock had climbed back up to $194.09. So, we missed out…

The bottom lines. You should use stop-loss orders. You need to protect yourself against losses so that you don't lose your shirt. But think about them carefully. The shorter time period over which you intend to hold the stock, the smaller the percentage you should be willing to risk, and vice versa. So, a day trader might use 1-5% while a long-term investor might use 15%. You will have to use a level that you're comfortable with. You'll have to sit down with each trade you make and calculate how much money you are willing to lose on the deal and then set your stop loss accordingly. Sometimes you're going to be wrong and miss out on a rebound but that's life. Now let's learn some basic concepts that are important in swing trading.

Trends

A big part of swing trading is recognizing trends in stocks, whether they are up or down. We will also want to look for points at which the trend will reverse. This works no matter how you're trading. If you are looking for long investments, then you're looking for the end of a downturn for buying opportunities, and peaks for selling opportunities. In other words, we are looking to buy low and sell high. If you are shorting the stock, then you'll be looking at the opposite trends.

Swing Traders Use Trends

To make money swing trading, you're going to utilize trends in order to get into a stock and determine when to exit the stock and book your profits. You are seeking to take advantage of a single move in the stock or a "swing" in the stock price. When a stock swings, then that means the opposing pressure is about to take over. So, you may be looking to exit your position. Alternatively, you may be looking for a good buying opportunity. The bottom line is that swing traders usually go with the prevailing trend. If you're bullish, you look for upward trends in the stock and book your profits on the upside. If you're bearish, then you're looking to capture gains on the downside.

Chapter 3. Why is Options Trading Worth the Risk?

At some point, you will need to take some loans so that you can expand your investment. Debt financing is attractive since the lending entity will not in any way dictate how you will use the credit. When a firm has a lot of pending debts in comparison with the operating cash as well as equity, it is highly leveraged. When a company's leverage is high, it, in turn, becomes sensitive to the economic changes. They too are subject to the risk of being bankrupt. The reason why leverage is riskier is that they are subject to;

Limited Growth

When you have a loan, the lending company will expect that you will pay in the period that was agreed upon when you were getting the loan. They hope that you will be on time and no failures should come along the way. It is a problem when an investor borrows money for a long-term project that will not generate some income immediately. That will make them find an alternative to how they will pay the loan to avoid breaching the contract. If the payment period has come, and the investor has no returns, paying the mortgage can be a burden in one way or the other. When you decide to start paying the loan, it will mean that you use the money you borrowed to pay back. When that happens, you will have less money for financing your operations. You will not be in a position to implement full on the plan that you had. That means that you can have retardation, and you will not execute your plan fully. When investing, you need a plan and to set deadlines for the completion so that you will remain on your focus. When you have to pay the loan with the money that you borrowed, you will not be in a position to hit your deadlines. That will mean that you will experience limited growth, and you may not have the potential to continue as per the plan.

Losing Assets

When you are unable to pay loans, and you are highly leveraged, that can lead to a conspirator of the assets that you have. There is no way that a company should pay capital sourcing from equity. When that happens, and the lender expects that you will pay your loan in time, they can decide to take some of your assets to stand in for the loan. The assets can be of a similar value or a value higher than your investment. When in a loan, the company is supposed to pay the lender before any other deductions. Repossession of assets can happen if there is no money to pay the lender in time. It the lender has to be paid even before the employees of the company, it means that the employees may look for another option and quit working with you. That will make you lose assets of value, and you will be left stranded.

Inability to Get More Financing

Before a lender gives you money to invest in any trade, they will first check out whether you have any other loan. They will do that to establish how secure their payment is with you. If you are in debt, no lender will want to lend you more because they are not sure whether you will be in a position to clear their debt. They will access the risk that is associated in case the company goes down, meaning there will be no one to pay their loan. When a company goes down, it is declared bankrupt, and that means that the lender cannot claim their money even on a legal basis. No lender will agree to put them last on your loan list since they know they will be the last to be paid.

An Investor Will Not Be in a Position to Attract Equity

When a company has high leverage, they are not able to increase the equity capital amount. And it is rare for an investor to give money to a business that has bid records of unclear loans. In the same way, lenders will avoid providing more money to a company with high amounts of investments, and the same way investors avoid such business. You will lose the potential of attracting investors when you have a lot of pending debts. When a lender knows they are the last in your line to be paid their loan, they will not find it comfortable to lend you. If at with any chance you get an investor to give you, they will demand a significant percentage in terms of ownership in return of borrowing you the money.

Multiple as Well as Constant Losses

There is a risk in leverage in cases where you invest in a particular stock and the price of the stock takes a negative change when you least expect. You will end up suffering a lot of losses since you have to pay the loan back in time and you have other expenses to deduct. That will be hard on you since there is no profit made considering you made a loss. Taking a loan can begin with the increase in losses as well as end with the losses locking in within a short period. High amounts of debts can get out of hand and can lead to bankruptcy at a very high speed. When you are declared bankrupt, it comes with several consequences. There is no time that you will get any other loan no matter how you will have an enticing business plan. No investor will want to have an association with a bankrupt person. That will make any investor who has the potential to fund you to pull out.

Even though you need a lot of money to invest in a long-term plan, you need to have an idea of how to repay the loan. The project you have May not at times work in the way you would want it to and the need to have a back-up plan. If it is necessary, avoid late payment of loans and maintain the discipline of the highest level when the repayment period arrives. If you observe all the rules layout when taking the loan, you will not have a hard time with the lender. They will be willing to lend you more and more when you need it.

Chapter 4. How to Get Started in Options Trading

You are required to have an idea of what generally is options trade. Take into consideration the various terminologies used in this field. This may include terms such as a holder, a writer, a striking place. Etc., it would be advisable to come up with a spreadsheet with these terminologies and make an effort to study them in-depth. This will contribute a lot to your understanding of what Option Trade revolves around. Generally, options trade can be defined as a contract that allows you to either buy or sell a stock at a certain strike price for a specified length of time. With this knowledge, you have already started making your steps towards Option Trading. You realize that options trading mostly revolves around the call option as well as the put option and hence the need to ensure that you understand what they entail in-depth. The options usually play a critical role; they control the value of the stock. You should also understand that the options are prone to expire, especially in cases where the contract is over. In this case, you end up losing your premiums to the developer.

When carrying on with how to start Options Trading, you will require to have brought together the necessary tools. This refers to various resources that will be sufficient enough to take you through the entire process of Option Trade. Your capital plays a very critical role in ensuring that you are able to purchase an option that best suits your strategy and be in a position to amerce as many profits as possible. In the cases where you plan on involving a broker, you can comfortably cater for their commissions as well as be in a position to hire their best services.

The other step that you must familiarize yourself with is the knowledge and understanding that options trade involves very high risks. The risks here are usually in two dimensions, the amount of money you lose as compared to the profits you would have realized, the other dimension is the probability of acquiring profits as compared to the probability of getting a loss. The high risks can occur, especially when the options have been purchased speculatively. If at one point you are not careful you might end up losing all your profits. You can easily acquire high profits if you have an in-depth understanding of the stock's price movement. Taking advantage of the options in such scenarios can go away up into protecting your investments beyond a reasonable doubt. In this case, you only stand to lose the premiums and a very small percentage of the investment, as you had depicted in the contract.

Getting to the most critical parts now, you will need to open a brokerage account either online or traditionally through a broker. Here there are various factors to consider before settling with the most reliable brokerage company. Ensure that you are aware of their costs and incentives, some of the brokerage companies may be offering discounts to their customers as a way of attracting them, and you can take advantage of this and benefit from the discounts they offer as well. You can also check on the conveniences and services that various brokerage companies offer before settling on either. These may be services such as money conversions or providing adequate information on the stock ratings. Having enumerated the pros and cons of each of the brokerage firms, then you can settle on one that best suits your desire. It is also advisable to ensure that your brokerage company has an acceptable form of money transfer, especially for online accounts. Some of the firms will provide you with Electronic Money Transfer systems hence enhancing convenience.

You can acquire the necessary approval application form your brokerage company before you can start buying options. You realize that most of the brokerage firms set limits for their customers; they usually do this so that they can prevent you from getting inappropriate risks that could have been avoided. They also do this as they too have their own interests that they are so much willing to protect, especially on matters to do with the legalities.

Familiarize yourself with the various technical analysis of options; you realize that options are usually short term. Failure to understand the resistance and support levels, the Fibonacci retracement, the importance of volume, and some basic knowledge of the moving averages will make it quite hard to go through the process with ease.

When you get into the actual trading, it would be inappropriate to start trading immediately. Instead, try to run some demo accounts and familiarize yourself with them for a period of one month. By doing this, you can try to evaluate your demo returns for some months and when you find some level of consistency in it. You can now gather the necessary confidence and start real trading. At least with these, you will have some basis under which you can base your analysis. By so doing, you will save yourself from suffering high risks as you are aware that in the demo account, there are no charges whatsoever that are involved.

When you get to trading now try as much as possible to avoid market prices since the may vary upon buying or selling the options. This may result in very high, but avoidable losses.

Ensure that you periodically reevaluate your strategy. This ensures that you learn on and on from any mistake that you may have committed during the trade. In the case where some of your strategies reap good returns, try as much as possible to utilize them while still trying to maximize their profitability. Ensure that you familiarize yourself with new market tactics that may seem quite profitable. You can also socialize with other people that are in the market who have strategies that may be doing better in the market than yours. This may as well build your confidence, especially after you suffer losses. Having like-minded people in the same field as you, to some extent, makes you confident in your own self such that you do not have to beat yourself after you make huge losses. They help you to move on and keep on track while at the same time checking on your strategy and making necessary adjustments wherever necessary. This union also gives you a sense of a community; with this, you are able to achieve a certain insight into the trade. Nonetheless, it would be wise of you remain quite focused on your strategies rather than diversifying so much on them. This saves you from going astray in your quest for new tactics that may, in the long run, fail.

Once you feel that you have familiarized yourself with your current trading strategies, you can try to get into some more complex strategies that in the long run, reap you higher profits if you get to understand them. When this is presented to you, do not be so overconfident to join the market without having to try a demo account for a couple of months, this will enable you to get a better understanding of how they run, with this you will be able to make a choice on whether to continue with your previous strategies or uphold the more complex ones. One of these strategies that you can actually try is the straddle strategy. In this strategy, you buy the call and the put option simultaneously; it appears as if it is a neutral options strategy.

Both the call and the put in this share the same strike price as well as the expiry date. In this case, you get your profits in the case where the prices either go above or below the strike price by an amount which is higher or rather more than that of the premium. This strategy is somewhat quite risky as it only applies when the market is moving up and down; otherwise, if it runs in the same direction, only that side will be exercisable.

Once you have fully mastered the art of handling even the complex strategies, do not stop there or lose sight, there is still more to learn. Try to maximize your profits as much as possible by familiarizing yourself with the metrics which other options traders use to reap more profits. They call it learning about the Greeks. In this case, you can use the metrics that take into account the profitability of profits. The profitability of profit refers to the opportunity of making at least a $0.01 profit on a given trade. The probability of profit is usually affected by aspects as buying options, selling options, or the overall reduction of stock or the time period. This would require a careful and in-depth insight to comprehend it fully and use it as your strategy to reap maximum benefits.

Chapter 5. Learning the Lingo

The first piece of terminology you have to grapple with is the concept of the premium. Despite the fancy name, the premium is simply the name given to the price of the contract. So why not call it the price? Well, this is because of the way the price arrives. Black-Scholes complexity aside, every option contract's premium has two components to it: the intrinsic value and the time value.

There is a third volatility value as well but let's ignore that for now. The intrinsic value is simply the difference between the price at which the option becomes valuable and the current price of the security. The time value is a price associated with how much time is left on the contract.

So at what price does the option become valuable? Well, this is called the strike price. The strike price is the threshold beyond which you can exercise the option. So if you buy a call (the right to buy) with a strike price of $10 and the current market price of the underlying is $5, your option has no intrinsic value since the strike price is above the market price.

Every contract has an expiration date with the most heavily traded ones being the ones expiring within a month. The time left for the option to expire is the key factor in determining how much time value the option has. If your call still has two months to expire, then there is a greater possibility of the market price exceeding the strike price, than if the option were expiring tomorrow.

Therefore, the former option would have a higher time value than the latter. Generally speaking, the closer you get to the expiration date, the lesser the time value is. The third factor in pricing is the volatility value. Briefly, the more volatile the underlying is, the greater this value.

Volatility refers to how far and how fast security moves. Volatile securities usually move very quickly and are thought of as being unpredictable thanks to their quick movements. Given this unpredictability, it is natural that the person selling you the option should be compensated for the risk they're undertaking.

The relation of the market price to the strike price has further terminology associated with it.

The reasoning behind this terminology is this. A call is valuable only when the market price increases beyond the strike price. Think about it. You're buying the option to give you the right to purchase the underlying. If the current market price is $5, the only calls that will make you a profit are those with strike prices below $5.

In anticipation of a rising market, traders often buy higher strike price options. So, if a trader buys a $10 strike price call, they're anticipating that the market will increase beyond this price before the option expires. Using this logic, can you figure out how the terminology works for a put? When is a put in the money?

Well, a put gives you the right to sell the underlying. So the only valuable puts will be the ones with a strike price higher than the current market price. Hence, with puts, when the strike price is greater than the market price, a put is said to be in the money. When the put's strike price is lower than the market price, it is out of the money. In other words, it is directly opposite to the call's conditions.

So what happens when you buy an option? Well, you pay the premium and then wait to see if you want to exercise it or not or sell if for a higher premium to someone else. You could also let it expire without doing anything. In all cases, the maximum size of your loss is limited to the premium you paid to buy the option.

I want to point out that irrespective of your trade moving into the money or not, you will forfeit the option premium. So when you enter an option trade, you're placing yourself at a loss right from the start. The good news is that this is your maximum loss. In a stock trade, your potential loss is the difference between the market price and zero, since every stock can turn worthless.

For example, if you buy AMZN at $246, your potential loss is -$246 per share. However, if you buy a call option, your maximum loss is the price of the option. If AMZN doesn't make it past the call's strike price, it doesn't matter for you since you don't own the stock and you don't have any obligation to buy it.

When you short a stock, that is, sell first before seeking to buy it back at a lower price, your potential loss is unlimited. This is because a stock can rise to infinite levels without stopping. If you shorted AMZN at $246, your potential loss is unlimited per share. It could rise to $1000, or $2000 and so on. Your maximum gain is $246 per share since it can only fall till zero.

However, if you buy a put option on AMZN, your maximum loss is capped at the option's premium while your maximum gain is capped at your option's price plus $246 since this is the maximum amount by which it could fall. The $246 will be added to the intrinsic value portion of the premium.

Here we see the major benefit of options which is their ability to cap your maximum risk. With stock trading, you can do this via a stop-loss order, but markets are notorious for jumping stop-loss levels due to liquidity concerns. Liquidity is a fundamental concept you need to understand to trade successfully.

Many traders, while first starting think that every price in the market will be honored and that transactions can occur at every level. This is not the case. Think of it as going to an actual market of say, fruits. If you want to sell your apples for $10, you will find a certain number of takers. If you want to sell it for $10,000, unless God blessed those apples personally, you're not going to find any takers.

There's no liquidity for apples at the $10,000 price. The same thing happens in the stock market all the time. When a stock moves violently, it often skips multiple levels, and it is quite common for an illiquid stock to skip right past the stop loss level. The broker can only execute your orders at the prevailing market price, so if that price happens to be multiple points lower than your stop loss, you have to eat the loss.

Chapter 6. Strike Price

The strike price is one of the most important if not the most important thing to understand when it comes to option contracts. The strike price will determine whether the underlying stock is actually bought or sold at or before the expiration date. When evaluating any options contract, the strike price is the first thing that you should look at. It's worth reviewing the concept and how it's utilized in the actual marketplace.

The strike price will let you home in on the profits that can be made on an options contract. It's the break-even point but also gives you an idea as to your profits and losses. Of course, the seller always gets the premium no matter what.

For a call contract, the strike price is the price that must be exceeded by the current market price of the underlying equity. For example, if the strike price is $100 on a call contract, and the current market price goes to any price above $100, then the purchaser of the call can exercise their right at any time to buy the stock. Then the stock can be disposed of with a profit. Suppose that the current price rises to $130. Then you can exercise your option to buy the stock at $100 a share, and then turn around and sell it on the market for $130 a share, making a $30 profit per share before taking into account the premium and other fees that might accrue with your trades. While as the buyer of the contract you have no obligations other than paying the premium, the seller is obligated no matter what, and they must sell you the shares at $100 per share no matter how much it pains them to see the $130 per share price. Of course, there are reasons behind the curtain that will explain why they would bother entering this kind of arrangement that we will explore later.

For a put contract, the strike price likewise plays a central role, but the value of the stock relative to the strike price works in the opposite fashion. A put is a bet that the underlying equity will decrease in value by a certain amount. Hence if the stock price drops below the strike price, then the buyer can exercise their right to sell the shares at the strike price even though the market price is lower. So, if your price is $100, if the current price of the equity drops to $80, the seller obligated to buy the 100 shares per contract from you at $100 a share even though the market price is $80 per share. In this case, you've made a gross profit of $20 a share.

The value of the strike price will not only tell you profitability but give you an indication of how much the stock must move before you are able to exercise your rights. Often when the amount is smaller, you might be better off.

When you know the strike price of different options contracts, then you can evaluate which one is better for you to buy.

Suppose that a stock is currently trading at $80 and you find two options put contracts. One has a strike price of $75 and the other has a strike price of $60. Further, let's suppose that both contracts expire at the same time. In the first case, the stock price in the market will need to drop just $5 before the contract becomes profitable. For the second contract, it will have to drop $20.

The potential worth of each contract per share is the difference. For the contract with the $75 strike price, that is only $5. For the second contract with the strike price of $60, the potential worth is $20, four times as much.

Determining which contract is better is a matter of analysis and taking some risk. You can't just go by face value, but you must take into consideration the expiration date together with an analysis of what the stock will actually do over that time period. It may be that it's going to be impossible for the stock to drop $20 in order to make the second contract valuable. If the expiration date comes before the stock drops that much in price, the contract will be worthless. In other words, you'd never be able to exercise your option of selling shares at strike amount. On the other hand, even though there is not much discrepancy between the strike and the market amount for the first contract, and the market price might only drop to say $70 per share, the chances of this happening before the expiration date is more likely.

Your analysis might be different if the contract with the lower strike price has a longer expiration date.

The lesson to take to heart is that a stock is more likely to move by smaller amounts over short time periods. But the higher the risk, the more the potential profits.

Chapter 7. Covered Calls

In this chapter, we'll investigate a trading strategy that is a good way to get started selling options for beginners. This strategy is called covered calls. By covered, we mean that you've got an asset that you own that covers the potential sale of the underlying stocks. In other words, you already own the shares of stocks. Now, why would you want to write a call option on stocks you already own? The basis of this strategy is that you don't expect the stock price to move very much during the lifetime of the options contract, but you want to generate money over the short term in the form of premiums that you can collect. This can help you generate a short-term income stream; you must structure your calls carefully.

Setting up covered calls is relatively low risk and will help you get familiar with many of the aspects of options trading. While it's probably not going to make you rich overnight, it's a good way to learn the tools of the trade.

Covered Calls involve a long position

In order to create a covered call, you need to own at least 100 shares of stock in one underlying equity. When you create a call, you're going to be offering potential buyers a chance to buy these shares from you. Of course, the strategy is that you're only going to sell high, but your real goal is to get the income stream from the premium.

The premium is a one-time non-refundable fee. If a buyer purchases your call option and pays you the premium, that money is yours. No matter what happens after that, you've got that cash to keep. In the event that the stock doesn't reach the strike price, the contract will expire, and you can create a new call option on the same underlying shares. Of course, if the stock price does pass the strike price, the buyer of the contract will probably exercise their right to buy the shares. You will still earn money on the trade, but the risk is you're giving up the potential to earn as much money that could have been earned on the trade.

You write a covered call option that has a strike price of $67. Suppose that for some unforeseen reason the shares skyrocket to $90 a share. The buyer of your call option will be able to purchase the shares from you at $67. So, you've gained $2 a share. However, you've missed out on the chance to sell the shares at a profit of $35 a share. Instead, the investor who purchased the call option from you will turn around and sell the shares on the markets for the actual spot price and they will reap the benefits.

However, you really haven't lost anything. You have earned the premium plus sold your shares of stock for a modest profit.

That risk – that the stocks will rise to a price that is much higher than the strike price - always exists, but if you do your homework, you're going to be offering stocks that you don't expect to change much in price over the lifetime of your call. So, suppose instead that the price only rose to $68. The price exceeded the strike price so the buyer may exercise their option. In that case, you are still missing out on some profit that you could have had otherwise, but it's a small amount and we're not taking into account the premium.

In the event that the stock price doesn't exceed the strike price over the length of the contract, then you get to keep the premium and you get to keep the shares. The premium is yours to keep no matter what.

In reality, in most situations, a covered call is going to be a win-win situation for you.

Covered Calls are a Neutral Strategy

A covered call is known as a "neutral" strategy. Investors create covered calls for stocks in their portfolio where they only expect small moves over the lifetime of the contract. Moreover, investors will use covered calls on stocks that they expect to hold for the long term. It's a way to earn money on the stocks during a period in which the investor expects that the stock won't move much at price and so have no earning potential from selling.

An Example of a Covered Call

Let's say that you own 100 shares of Acme Communications. It's currently trading at $40 a share. Over the next several months, nobody is expecting the stock to move very much, but as an investor, you feel Acme Communications has solid long-term growth potential. To make a little bit of money, you sell a call option on Acme Communications with a strike price of $43. Suppose that the premium is $0.78 and that the call option lasts 3 months.

For 100 shares, you'll earn a total premium payment of $0.78 x 100 = $78. No matter what happens, you pocket the $78.

Now let's say that over the next three months the stock drops a bit in price so that it never comes close to the strike price, and at the end of the three-month period, it's trading at $39 a share.

The options contract will expire, and it's worthless. The buyer of the options contract ends up empty-handed. You have a win-win situation. You've earned the extra $78 per 100 shares, and you still own your shares at the end of the contract.

Now let's say that the stock does increase a bit in value. Over time, it jumps up to $42, and then to $42.75, but then drops down to $41.80 by the time the options contract expires. In this scenario, you're finding yourself in a much better position. In this case, the strike price of $43 was never reached, so the buyer of the call option is again left out in the cold. You, on the other hand, keep the premium of $78, and you still get to keep the shares of stock. This time since the shares have increased in value, you're a lot better off than you were before, so it's really a win-win situation for YOU, even though it's a losing situation for the poor soul who purchased your call.

Sadly, there is another possibility, that the stock price exceeds the strike price before the contract expires. In that case, you're required to sell the stock. You still end up in a position that isn't all that bad, however. You didn't lose any actual money, but you lost a potential profit. You still get the premium of $78, plus the earnings from the sale of the 100 shares at the strike price of $43.

A covered call is almost a zero-risk situation because you never actually lose money even though if the stock price soars, you obviously missed out on an opportunity. You can minimize that risk by choosing stocks you use for a covered call option carefully. For example, if you hold shares in a pharmaceutical company that is rumored to be announcing a cure for cancer in two months, you probably don't want to use those shares for a covered call. A company that has more long-term prospects but probably isn't going anywhere in the next few months is a better bet.

How to go about creating a covered call

To create a covered call, you'll need to own 100 shares of stock. While you don't want to risk a stock that is likely to take off in the near future, you don't want to pick a total dud either. There is always someone willing to buy something – at the right price. But you want to go with a decent stock so that you can earn a decent premium.

You start by getting online at your brokerage and looking up the stock online. When you look up stocks online, you'll be able to look at their "option chain" which will give you information from a table on premiums that are available for calls on this stock. You can see these listed under bid price. The bid price is given on a per share basis, but a call contract has 100 shares. If your bid price is $1.75, then the actual premium you're going to get is $1.75 x 100 = $175.

An important note is that the further out the expiration date, the higher the premium. A good rule of thumb is to pick an expiry that is between two and three months from the present date. Remember that the longer you go, the higher the risk because that increases the odds that the stock price will exceed the strike price and you'll end up having to sell the shares.

You have an option (no pun intended) with the premium you want to charge. Theoretically, you can set any price you want. Of course, that requires a buyer willing to pay that price for you to actually make the money. A more reasonable strategy is to look at prices people are currently requesting for call options on this stock. You can do this by checking the asking price for the call options on the stock. You can also see prices that buyers are currently offering by looking at the bid prices. For an instant sale, you can simply set your price to a bid price that is already out there. If you want to go a little bit higher, you can submit the order and then wait until someone comes along to buy your call option at the bid price.

To sell a covered call, you select "sell to open."

Benefits of Covered Calls

•   A covered call is a relatively low-risk option. The worst-case scenario is that you'll be out of your shares but earn a small profit, a smaller profit than you could have made if you had not created the call contract and simply sold your shares. However, you also get the premium.

•   A covered call allows you to generate income from your portfolio in the form of premiums.

•   If you don't expect any price moves on the stock in the near term and you plan on holding it long term, it's a reasonable strategy to generate income without taking much risk.

Risks of Covered Calls

• Covered calls can be a risk if you're bullish on the stock, and your expectations are realized, and there is a price spike. In that case, you've traded the small amount of income of the premium with a voluntary cap of the strike price for the potential upside you could have had if you had simply held the stock and sold it at the high price.

• If the stock price plummets, while you still get the premium, the stocks will be worthless unless they rebound over the long term. You shouldn't use a call option on stocks that you expect to be on the path to a major drop in the coming months. In that case, rather than writing a covered call, you should simply sell the stocks and take your losses. Alternatively, you can continue holding the stocks to see if they rebound over the long term.

Chapter 8. Strategy for Selling Covered Calls

There's a whole list of considerations that you will eventually want to bear in mind as you expand your knowledge and develop your own, personal strategy. Every trader has a different attitude towards what works and what doesn't – there are plenty of ways to make selling a covered call work, but you'll probably find yourself preferring one or two strategies.

We'll take a look now at those considerations in more detail to guide you as you delve into the covered call more deeply:

- The Market Environment: You are no doubt aware that traders of stocks and shares are happy in a bull market and disgruntled in a bear market. You may also know that such traders hate a flat market most of all, because very little is happening and there aren't many big profits to be made. For you, as a seller of covered calls, the opposite is true. I highly recommend waiting for the market to temporarily flatten before embarking on a spate of covered call sales. This is because you're only really interested in small changes to your share prices – if they are skyrocketing, you're losing more money on your contract. There also isn't as much danger of the bottom falling out of the market and your stock prices plummeting at the same time, which would be problematic.

- Your Underlying Stock: There is nothing more important to your success than choosing the right stocks to invest in in the first place. I cannot stress strongly enough that your success will be heightened if you pick stocks that move up very slowly. You don't want stocks that rise and fall very quickly, especially as a beginner, because they have a habit of making surprising moves that ruin your strategy. If they drop too far, you stand to lose a lot of money in the sale; if they rise too high, you lose the money you could have made if you'd sold them at that price. Traders who deal in risk often enjoy these stocks because they have higher premiums and a chance for huge profits, but that goes against the idea of selling covered calls: you're looking for a steady income that will underpin your riskier strategies elsewhere. By all means go for the riskier stock elsewhere in your strategy, but avoid it like the plague for this particular function.

- The Premium: Always remember that the premium is your guaranteed profit. Whatever else happens, you're going to walk away with that cash. When you factor in the cost to list the option and any commission you will lose to your broker, you'll be able to calculate the actual profit you'll make on that premium. Set yourself a minimum premium – a number that you consider to be enough to provide a profit you'll be happy with, on the assumption that it's the only profit you make. When you move ahead on setting the strike price, you'll likely adjust this base figure up or down based on what you think the underlying stock is going to do before the expiration date. Remember that the premium is only one component of the overall profit you will make – if you then set a strike price that means you lose the same amount of cash on selling the shares as you made through the premium, the trade wasn't worth doing in the first place.

- The Expiration Date: There's a reason that the premiums on covered calls get higher the further out the expiration date. It's because, much like the weather forecasts we all deride on a daily basis, it gets harder and harder to predict what's going to happen to a share price the further out you go. Also bear in mind that your money is going to be tied up until the expiration date, so the premium will increase as a nod to that sacrifice. Most investors believe that a time span of between a month and three months works best.

- The Strike Price: You might think that the strike price you set should be based on what you, as the seller, are comfortable with, but actually it's the opposite. You're looking for a strike price that your buyer will feel comfortable with, because otherwise they aren't going to buy. That, in turn, is going to be dictated by the expiration date you set, as well as the premium you're asking for and how stable or volatile the underlying stock is. Your best bet is to put yourself in the shoes of your buyer: would you purchase that contract? How much would you stand to gain? Set your strike price accordingly and then take a look at it from your own point of view. Would this be an acceptable profit for you? If so, you've hit the nail on the head.

With all these factors in mind, you are likely starting to see that there is no single "correct decision" when it comes to selling covered calls. It's going to take practice and concentration to figure out which ones work best for you.

It's also important to note that your strategy is probably going to change as you gain experience. The more options you sell, the more you will see new and more advanced ways to take advantage of the market. For now, I urge you to be conservative in your approach and accept that selling covered options is not going to win you your fortune – but it is going to help you increase the seed money you have available to do just that.

Outcomes of a Covered Sell

As we're using the idea of selling covered calls as a trade example to help you learn the basics of option trading overall, let's now take a close look at what is going to happen to your option once you've listed it.

- The stock increases in value: If the stock moves up and hits your strike price, this means that your buyer can now exercise their right and buy the shares. The more it rises, the more likely that the buyer will do exactly that. When your goal is to sell shares, this is what you want to happen – and you will pocket the premium as well as, of course, the difference between the shares as they were valued when you listed them and the value they are at on the expiration date (in other words, capital gains).

- The stock value doesn't move: If the shares don't change either up or down during the time the option is open, then they won't hit the strike price and you won't have to sell. You will pocket the premium and can factor it into your overall profits when you relist the stock. Many options traders actually count on this outcome – it's the one they are hoping for because it means they make a profit AND keep the shares. Feel free to follow the same logic, but make sure your entire plan doesn't hinge on it. You don't control the market, so you could find yourself met by a nasty surprise.

- The stock drops in value: If this happens, the outcome is very similar to the share price not moving at all. The difference is that you are losing money on the shares themselves all the time they are dropping. They might bounce back, but if they don't then the expiration date will arrive and you'll be holding shares that are now worth a lot less than they used to be, which constitutes a loss. If, while monitoring your option contracts, you see that a stock is starting to drop, you need to prepare to take emergency action. Do this by calculating your "breakeven" price: subtract the premium per share from the price of the share at the time you listed it. For example, if the share was worth $50 and the premium per share is $1.50, your breakeven price per share is $48.50. If it falls below this price, you have the option to buy back your option – not something you should rely on or do often, but good as an emergency action. To do this, go back to the order entry and select "Buy to Close". Enter either the current ask price or something lower, depending how risky you want to be. Once the trade goes through, you are back in control of your shares and can either keep or sell them, as you deem fit.

As an aside, you should know that buying back your options is actually a deliberate strategy used by some people who trade in covered calls. Doing so allows you to manage your own risk, ending trades that are likely to be disadvantageous for you so that you can list those stocks again at a later date.

For instance, let's say that your underlying stock is rising fast and you think you're going to lose out on a lot of potential profit as it continues to skyrocket. You could "roll up" your options by buying back your call at the current ask price or lower and then selling them again at a higher strike price.

Simply setting your stock to sell is enough to garner you a regular income to support your options trading, but there are other ways you can make the most of the market.

A typical strategy for a person who deals in selling covered calls is to purchase a stock and sell a covered call on that stock at the exact same time. It's called a "Buy-Write Strategy". Your brokerage firm will almost certainly allow you to do this and may even have it listed on their online order screen for you to select.

So what would you be looking for if you did this?

- A stock that you would be happy to have in your share portfolio, assuming that the buyer never realized their right to purchase it.
- A stock that is showing a premium rate on the marketplace you would be happy to accept.
- A stock that is predictable in that it is rising or dipping in worth slowly over time.

Keep your eyes firmly on the stock market over time and you will start to see those trends. You'll also develop an eye for spotting good trades – the ones where you can make a quick profit by selling a few contracts at a good premium price.

A second advanced strategy is to use options trading to get rid of stocks you don't want to own any more. Maybe, for instance, they've been flat for a long time and you aren't seeing enough movement to make them worthwhile. You can set up a sell that would return a good premium while allowing you to get rid of your stocks at close to their current price. Instead of simply unloading them, you'd walk away with the premium as a potentially tidy profit.

Thirdly, you can choose to use the "half and half" strategy: keep some of your stocks in a particular company and sell the rest. This works well if you aren't really sure whether you should sell them all, but make sure you are keeping records of what you have done.

Stepping Up a Tier: Buying Calls

We're ready to move on to the more sophisticated areas of options trading. You have tested the waters, made a little cash and you feel comfortable with the mechanics of the market. Now, you can start actually buying those calls and hopefully begin to make some real money as you do.

It's actually a simpler business to buy a call, in terms of physically going ahead and doing so. However, it's not quite so easy to make a profit. You're going to need to start small and dedicate yourself to the learning curve – and you need to understand that there is a risk involved in buying calls, so you don't want to stake your life savings on your efforts.

Let me take the opportunity to advise you to build up slowly over time rather than jump straight in with a hundred buys in a single day. Be circumspect about your actions: a small profit is better than no profit at all. Save your riskiest ideas for when you've set up a nest egg through your sells and you feel confident enough in your own judgment that you're as sure as it's possible to be that your risk will pay off.

As a reminder, what you are actually doing when you buy a call is purchasing the right to buy the underlying stock if it reaches the strike price before the deadline. You aren't obligated to buy it – if you choose not to, all you have lost is the premium you paid for that right.

The best-case scenario for you, as the buyer, is that the stock suddenly starts rising at a high speed before the deadline arrives. You want it to go beyond the strike price so that, when it comes time to exercise your right, you are purchasing your stock at a lower rate than it is now worth. Obviously, you then have the option to instantly list that stock as a covered sell, which would allow you to realize that profit in real money.

That final piece of the puzzle is the important one. As an options trader, you are not in the business of building a stock portfolio. You don't really want to actually own those shares – you want to make a profit on them as they pass through your hands. You want to buy them for less than they are worth and then sell them on, perhaps even for more than they are worth if you are lucky. It's within that transaction your money will be made.

Buying calls has several advantages for you as an options trader:

- It doesn't cost much to get involved in the movement of a particular stock. You only need fork out the amount for the premium, after which you can sit back and wait to see what the stock does before making your purchase decision based on actual information, rather than on speculating what the market will do.

- It allows you to make use of the kinds of "tips" that market experts have a bad habit of swearing by. You read the news, you're watching the markets and you have information that makes you think a certain stock is about to rise fast and hard. You want to take advantage of that, obviously, and options trading allows you to do so much more safely than simply buying the stock. If you're wrong, you'll only lose your premium and you may even make a small profit. If you were wrong and purchased the stock and then it plummeted rather than rose, you stand to lose a whole lot more cash.

One thing to note before you start buying calls is that you'll want to wait for the right time. You are no longer interested in a flat market – this time you want a bull market where stock prices are rising.

What you are looking for is an underlying stock you have faith in – you think it's going to rise in value over the next few months. Let's say you've found a stock that's currently at $50 and you believe it will continue to rise steadily. Predicting the rate of its growth, you think it will be at $80 in two months' time.

What you would be looking for in that scenario is a call contract that would allow you to purchase shares for LESS than the $80 you think they will rise to at that time. You must also juggle the math to make sure that you will not be paying a premium that would wipe out the profit you would make.

For example, you might find a contract option that will allow you to buy the stock at $80 per share on the deadline, with a premium of $1 per share. You think the stock is actually going to be worth $85 on that date, so you would actually be making a profit of $4 per share. Had the premium been $5, you'd have made no profit at all.

Chapter 9. Call Spreads

If the prospect of implementing the long stock leg of the previous strategies intimidated you, you're going to love this chapter. This is because call spreads do not need you to establish a stock position. Instead, you will be playing one strike price against another. The downside is that you need to have a definite market bias, so they aren't fully market neutral from a strategy perspective.

Truth be told none of the strategies are 100% market neutral. However, from a risk perspective, they insulate you from the gyrations of the market, and this is the context in which you should understand these strategies. So let's take a look at how call spreads work.

Bull Call Spread Strategy

The bull call spread assumes that you have a bullish view on the market based on your technical analysis. The beauty of this strategy is that it can be adjusted, just like a collar but without the need for establishing a long stock position. Indeed, all spread strategies have this inherent advantage to them.

This strategy works best in markets which are titled bullish but not explicitly so. What I mean is that often the market heads in a particular direction, but you'll find that it meanders about, diving as often as it rises with a small net push upwards. This sort of see-saw movement is perfect for the bull call spread.

It works even in strong bull markets, although personally, I recommend simply going long on a call to capture the full movement. Mind you, such strong bullish movements happen very infrequently, so you need to pick and choose carefully. Let's take a deeper look at how this strategy works.

Execution

The bull call spread has two legs to it:

1. A long at or in the money call
2. A short out of the money call

The primary profit generator in this strategy is the long call. This is what captures the upward movement of the stock and enables you to earn the increased premium via the increased intrinsic value of the option. The short call is effectively your profit target, or slightly beyond it and increases your overall profit and you earn income from the premium upon writing it.

Let's look at how the math works out using good old AMZN. Our market price is still $1833.51 so to establish the first leg of this trade, let's choose an in the money or at the money option, from the near month contracts. The closest we can get is 1835, which is being offered at $63.65 per share.

Next, what would be an appropriate target price? Well, this depends on how you read the market. If it is ranging sideways, but with a slightly bullish title, placing your target at the range boundary is a good idea. Obviously, your short call will need to be beyond this limit. Let's say our target is $1862. This makes writing the 1865 strike call an attractive option. The premium we will receive on writing the option is $44.55 per share.

So how does the math work out?

Cost of trade entry = Cost of long call - Premium from short call = 63.65-44.55 = $19.10 per share.

Maximum gain = Short call strike price - long call strike price = 1865-1835 = $30 per share.

Maximum loss = cost of trade entry.

Your trade entry equals the maximum possible loss because if the price of the stock decreases, as a worst-case scenario, your long call expires worthless and you get to keep the full premium from the short call. Your maximum profit is capped by the strike price of the short call.

Note that you need not be worried about the short call moving into the money. This is because you have the lower long call covering this position. In such a scenario, you simply exercise the lower call and use that to fulfill the higher call's exercise.

The reward to risk ratio of this particular example is pretty decent if not amazing.

Remember that this strategy takes advantage of sluggish markets or non-committal markets with a slight bullish tilt to them. In such markets, a directional trader stands a very high chance of being wiped out. Viewed in this light, the advantage of this strategy is obvious.

Adjustment

It is possible to adjust the bull call spread. Again, this depends on how confident you are in your analysis, and if you believe that the market is faking traders out before going in its intended direction. The adjustment is the same as with a collar. First, you cover your short call position for a profit, since its premium would have decreased.

Next, you close out the long call for a loss since it will now be out of the money. All things being equal, the loss from the long call will be offset by the gain from closing the short call. So on a net basis, you're still in the trade. You reestablish a long call from the new market level and can decide whether you wish to keep the same target price or change it.

Notice how, unlike the collar, there is no absolute need for price to hit its target. This is because you do not have the long stock component in the trade which will carry an unrealized loss when the market dips. You simply square out your calls and reestablish the trade. If you feel you made a bad call, you eat the maximum loss and move on.

Risk management underpins the success of this strategy. You should evaluate your ability to read the markets beforehand, and I'll give you a framework within which you can improve and analyze your abilities. Once you've established your success rate, you can then work out how much you need to risk, given the reward on offer.

You can always use leverage to finance this trade, but it doesn't make it easier to enter the trade as it does with the collar. As with all things leverage, be careful and check that it squares with your risk math. With this strategy, the most obvious advantage is the lack of upfront margin needed. This makes it a much more approachable and realistic strategy for those traders who don't have large amounts of capital to risk trading.

In case you turn out to be completely wrong about the market direction, you can always adapt and turn the strategy around to account for this. The way to do this is to establish a bear call spread.

Bear Call Spread Strategy

Just like the bull call spread takes advantage of sluggish bull markets, strategy takes advantage of sluggish bear markets. The best time to put both of these strategies into action is towards the end of trends where counter trend participation is getting higher by the minute. The market is about to move into an accumulative or distributive phase in preparation of a trend change.

This happens to be the state of the market for the most part so you can rest assured that both of these strategies will work wonders for you. The bear call spread also works in a sideways market with the best place of implementing it is near the top end of a sideways range. For now, let's dive in and break this down.

Execution

The bear call spread contains two legs within it:

1. An at the money or near the money short call
2. An out of the money long call

The primary instrument of profit is the short call which takes advantage of the price decreasing while the long call caps the downside. The primary earning factor in this trade is the premium you will earn on writing the short call. Similar to the bull call, your maximum profit and loss are capped, and this gives you a great view of your trade's probabilities right off the bat.

Let's look at how this would work with the current levels of AMZN. With a market price of $1833.50, the closest at the money call in the far month is the 1835 strike call. Writing this earns us a premium of $60.15 per share (the bid price of the contract). When it comes to deciding the strike price of the long call, you want to place this beyond the closest relevant resistance level. Let's say this happen to be the 1840 level. The premium for this happens to be $58.10 per share.

So let's look at how the math will work out:

Cost of trade entry = Cost of long call - Premium earned from short call = 58.1-60.15 = -$2.05 (you earn this amount on entry)

Maximum loss = Strike price of long call - Strike price of short call = 1840- 1835 = $5 per share.

Maximum gain = cost of trade entry.

The maximum gain you can earn on this trade is from the premium of the short call. However, your long call will decrease in price simultaneously so they will offset one another. As you can see, the reward/risk profile is skewed for this strategy with the risk being greater than the reward.

So why should you pursue this? Well, first of all, you must understand that the success rate of this strategy depends a lot on how well you can read market conditions. If the market is strongly bearish, you're better off buying a put instead of using the bear call spread. Again, it is the fact that you can produce profits in sluggish markets that makes it so attractive.

Most directional trades get wiped out in the sideways market or stay out entirely because if the market doesn't go anywhere, how can they make money. This is not the case with options, so an inverted reward to risk profile is a small price to pay. As always, your risk management is paramount, and you should work out your numbers well in advance.

Adjustment

Can you adjust this trade? Sure. Just like the bull call spread, if the market goes against you, you move the spread higher and have your initial legs offset one another by closing them out or exercising them. Or you could absorb the maximum loss and move on.

The real question here is whether you should adjust a bear spread to a bull spread and vice versa.

Calendar Call Spread Strategy

The spreads we've seen thus far have been what are called vertical spreads. This implies how they show up on the option chain, where strike prices are listed on top of one another. By shorting one and buying another, you're earning the difference in the prices of the two and hence the term' spread'.

Vertical spreads require you to trade options within the same expiration month but horizontal spreads, which is what the calendar spread is, involves buying and selling options form different expiration months. The call calendar spread is a bullish strategy that can be used to great effect as we'll see.

Execution

The calendar call spread consists of two legs:

1. A current month or short term short call
2. A near month or longer-term long call

The idea is that while the stock takes its time to make it to the longer (time frame) call's strike price, you might as well collect the premium on the short call in the meantime. The instrument for profit is the longer call which captures the upward movement in the stock.

The longer term call can be from the near month or something from the longer cycle. The choice is yours. The only consideration here is the liquidity since you don't want to be trading in an instrument which has a huge spread thanks to low demand or trading volume. As long as the liquidity is fine and spreads are low or manageable, you should be fine.

As your first step to implementing the trade, you will purchase an at or in the money call in anticipation of the move upwards. The short call is at a level you think the price is not going to reach within that time frame. The idea is to earn the premium from the short call and the capital gain from the long call. If this trade works out, it is as close to a win-win as you can get in the markets. Let's see how the math works with AMZN.

Let's say our long call is from the near month. The price we'll pay for the 1830 call, which is the one nearest to market price and in the money is $63.65. For our short call, let's say there a medium level resistance at 1840, which AMZN is going to have to work to get past and is unlikely to do this by the end of the month.

The premium we earn on this call is $36.30.

The cost of entry = Cost of long call - premium earned from short call = 63.65-36.3 = $27.35 per share.

Maximum loss = cost of entry

There are many scenarios for calculating the maximum gain as you can imagine since this depends on whether the short term call ever moves into the money. Whatever the scenario, you will have to subtract your cost of entry from the final gain.

Horizontal spreads are thus different from vertical spreads thanks to their open-ended nature. It will take some getting used to, but with time, you'll find that they tend to be far more rewarding if you can get your analysis correct.

Switching Strategies

To paraphrase Spider-man's uncle, with flexibility, comes great responsibility. You have the freedom to change strategies on the fly without closing out your positions for huge losses when it comes to options trading. However, just because you can doesn't mean you should switch. This is especially true for beginners.

What happens most often is that traders misread the range and end up implementing these strategies in the exact opposite phases of the market. For example, a bear call spread is best implemented in or at the end of a distributive phase. There are some very simple and specific guidelines you can follow to determine these but traders will move in unprepared nonetheless thanks to greed.

Really, the major cause of losses and unrestricted switching is greed and a lack of being prepared. So if this happens to you, take some time away from the market and evaluate yourself. Sometimes, despite being well prepared, the market just doesn't go in your favor. In such cases, you should flip your bias and go the other way, as long as overall market conditions support this action.

Remember that throughout all of the calculations I've given you, I haven't included the cost of taxes and commissions. These can add up to a massive amount if you trade regularly and place a threshold which you will find difficult to jump over ("Day Trading Taxes - How profits on trading are taxed," 2019). Often, day traders need to make 100% on their trades to break even. This is the effect commissions have on trading so you should not underestimate their effect no matter how small they may be.

Having given you the doomsday speech, it's only fair that I should also highlight that such flexibility is not available to those who trade directionally. Options enable you to switch your views on the market in an instant and align yourself perfectly with prevalent sentiment so if the opportunity arises and the conditions support it, don't hesitate to flip your bias and go the other way.

Of course, there's also the flexibility to change the shape of your spread from vertical to a horizontal one. All of these options (pun intended) can make your head spin at the moment, so the best way to approach this is to decide upon a single strategy of adjustment. See how it works out for you and then slowly see if you can incorporate another.

It's easier to change strategies within vertical spreads as opposed to converting a vertical spread to a horizontal one or a horizontal spread with the opposite bias. Take baby steps with this and above all else, make sure you understand how your risk math changes with each adjustment. This involves understanding how your success rate will change and how the change will impact your reward to risk numbers.

One important thing to keep in mind is that you need statistical relevance with your data when evaluating switching strategies. The easiest way of gathering as much data as possible is to use a dummy trading or paper trading platform and rack up as many trades as you can in a short while. Software such as Ninjatrader will help you do this.

Chapter 10.   Buying Calls

Buying calls is a more advanced form of training than selling covered calls. But it's not that complicated, so let's dive in.

What you're actually buying

Remember that one option contract is for 100 shares, so you'll need to be able to buy 100 shares of the stock in order to exercise your right to buy.

Also, remember that an options contract has a deadline. If the stock price fails to exceed the strike price by the deadline, you're out of luck and will lose whatever money that you invested in the premium. In relative terms, the premium price will be small so chances are if you are careful and not starting out by buying large numbers of options contracts, you won't be out that much money.

Your Goal Buying Options Contracts

The goal when purchasing options contracts is to buy a stock at a price that is lower than its current market value. In other words, you want the stock price to be significantly higher than the strike price so that you're enjoying significant savings in purchasing the stock. When evaluating your options, you'll need to take into account the added costs of the premium paid plus commissions. In some cases, commissions can be substantial so make sure you know what they are ahead of time so that you choose a good strike price and exercise your options at the right time.

You're a trader, not an investor

You may be mentally conditioned to think in terms of investing. An investor wants to build a diversified portfolio over a long time period that they believe will increase in value over the long term. A trader operates in the same universe but has different goals. You are after short term profits – not investments. You are not going to hold this stock. If you were interested in holding the stock, you would simply buy it at the lower price that is currently on offer. Your goal is to be able to buy at the strike price when the stock has increased significantly in price and then sell it immediately so that you can pocket the profits.

Let's take an example. Suppose that XYZ corporation is currently selling at $30 a share. People are expecting the stock to rise, and some people are really bullish about its short-term prospects. If you are an investor, your goal is to get the stock at the lowest possible price and then hold it long term. If you are using strategies like dollar cost averaging, you might be buying a few shares every month without paying too much attention to what the price is specifically on the day you purchase. In any case, as an investor, you'll simply buy the shares at $30.

As a trader, you're hoping to cash in on the moves of XYZ over the next couple of months. You'll buy an options contract, let's say its premium is $0.90 and the strike price is $35. Your cost for the 100 shares is $90.

Then the stock price shoots up to $45. Since it passed the strike price, you can exercise your option to buy the shares at the strike price. You can buy them at $35 for a total price of $3,500. But remember – you're not an investor in for the long haul. You'll immediately unload the shares. You sell the shares for $4,500 and make a $1,000 profit. After considering your premium, your profit is $910. It will go a little bit lower after considering commissions, but you get the idea. The purpose of buying call options is to make fast profits on stocks you think are going to spike.

It's hard to guess when the best time is to really buy call options. Obviously, you don't want to do it when a major recession hit. The optimal time is during a bull market, or when a specific company is expected to hit on something big, that will suddenly increase its value in the markets. A good time to look is also when a recession hits, but it passes the bottom out period.

Benefits of Buying Call Options

Call options have many benefits that we've already touched on earlier. In Particular:

- Call options allow you to control 100 shares of stock without actually investing in the 100 shares – unless they reach a price where you get the profit that you want.
- Call options allow you to sit and wait, patiently watching the market before making your move.
- If your bet doesn't work out, you're only going to lose a small amount of money on the contract. In our example, if XYZ loses value, and ends up at $28 per share instead of moving past your strike price of $35, then you're only out the $90 you paid for the premium.
- Call buying provides a way to leverage expensive stock.

What to look for when buying Call options

Now let's take a look at some factors that you'll be on the lookout for when buying call options. You're going to want to be able to purchase shares of the stock you're interested in at a price that is less than the price you think it will go up to. You need to do this in order to ensure that the stock price surpasses the strike price. Of course, it's impossible to know what the future holds so this will involve a bit of speculation. You'll have to do a lot of reading and research to make educated guesses on where you expect the stock to go in the next few weeks or months.

Second, you'll need to take into account the cost of the premium when making your estimates. For the sake of simplicity, suppose that you find a call option with a premium of $1 per share. You're going to need a strike price that is high enough to take that into account. If you go for a stock that is $40 a share with a $1 premium and a strike price of $41, obviously you're not going to make anything unless the stock price goes higher than $41.

Remember that exercising your rights on the options contract is not a path toward immediate money. You're going to have to turn around and sell it ASAP in order to profit. Of course, when you sell is a judgment call as is when you exercise your right to buy. You're going to want to wait until the right moment to buy, but its impossible to really know what that right moment is. This is where trading experience helps and even then, the most skilled experts can make mistakes. For a beginner, the best thing to do is exercise your right to buy the shares and then sell them as soon as they've gone far enough past the strike price for you to make a profit and cover the premium. If you wait too long, there is always the chance that the stock price will start declining again, and it will go below your strike price and never exceed it again before the contract expires.

Open Interest

If you get online to check stocks you're interested in, one of the measures you will see is "Open Interest." This tells you the number of open or outstanding derivative contracts there are for that particular stock. Every time that a buyer and seller enter into an options contract, this value increases by one. What you want to do with open interest as a trader looking to make real cash from call options is to look for stocks that show big movement in the number of open trades. You're going to want to look for increasing numbers. This means that other traders have an interest in buying call options on this stock and that they're expecting it to go up in value in the near future.

Of course, you're going to want to take an educated approach to this. Simply getting online and going through random stocks will be a waste of time, it might take you weeks to find something.

You're going to want to prepare ahead of time by keeping an eye on the financial news. Watch Fox Business, read the Wall Street Journal, and watch CNBC and read any other financial publications that are to your liking. Find out what stocks the experts are talking about and which ones they expect to make significant moves over the next few weeks and months. Keep in mind these people and experts often make mistakes, so you're only using it as a guideline. You also don't want to focus solely on looking for stocks that are going to make moves; you want to keep up with company news. You need to keep your ears open for news such as the development of a new drug or the latest electronic gadget. Sometimes you might find out news about that before the stock begins attracting a lot of interest in the markets.

Tips for Buying Call Options

- Don't buy a call option with a strike price that you don't think the stock can beat.
- Always include the premium price in your analysis.
- Look for calls that are just in the money. These are likely to bring a modest profit.
- Call options that are out of the money might give you an option for a cheaper premium.
- However, the premium shouldn't be your primary consideration when looking to buy a call option. Compared to the money required to buy the shares and the potential profits if the stock goes past the strike price, the premium is going to be a trivial cost in most cases – provided of course the strike price is high enough to take the premium into account.
- Look at the time value. If you're looking for larger profits, it's better to aim for longer contracts.

Remember, that with any call option you have the option to buy the stock at the strike price at any time between today's date and the deadline when the stock market price exceeds the strike price. Longer time frames mean you increase the chances of that happening. Even if the price goes a little above the strike price and dips down, with a longer window of time before the deadline, you can wait and see if it rebounds. Remember if it never does, you're only out the premium.

- Start small. Beginning traders shouldn't bet the farm on options. You'll end up broke if you do that. The better approach is to start by investing in one contract at a time and gaining experience as you go.

Chapter 11. Trading Varying Time Frames

Weekly Options Trading

Weekly options are listings which provide an opportunity for short-term trading as well as plenty of hedging possibilities. As the name states, they have an expiration time of exactly one week; in general, they are listed on Thursday and expire the following Friday. While they have been around for decades, in the past they have primarily been the domain of investors who work with cash indices. This level of exclusivity changed in 2011 when the Chicago Board of Options expanded the number of ways they could be traded, especially to make them more easily acceptable to traders like you. Since then, the number of stocks that can be traded weekly has grown from 28 to nearly 1,000.

In addition to having a short time frame, weekly options differ from traditional options in that they are only available 3 weeks out of the month. They are also never listed in the monthly expiration style. In fact, the week that monthly options expire, they are technically the same as weekly options.

Advantages of weekly options: The biggest benefit of buying into weekly options is the fact you are free to purchase exactly what you need for the exact trade you are looking to make without having to worry about coming up with extra capital or dealing with more options than you currently need. This means if you are looking to start a swing trade, or even an intraday trade, weekly options will have you covered. For those looking to sell, weekly options provide the ability to do so more frequently, rather than having to wait a month between sales.

Weekly options trades are also useful in that they lead to reduced costs for trades that have longer spreads, such as diagonal spreads or calendar spreads as they can sell weekly options against them. They are also useful to higher volume trades as they are useful when it comes to hedging larger positions and portfolios against potential risky events. Also, when the market is range bound the weekly options, market can still be utilized through means such as the iron butterfly or iron condor.

Disadvantages: The biggest disadvantage when it comes to weekly options is the fact that you will not ever have very much time for a trade to turn around if you make the wrong choice in the first place. If you are selling options, then you will also need to know that their gamma will also be much more sensitive than it would be with more traditional options. This means that if you are planning to short options, then a relatively small move overall can still lead to an out of the money option entering into the money very quickly.

Weekly options are also known to require a good deal more micromanaging of risk. Without taking the time to size your trades and guarantee your profits properly, you will find that your available trade balance disappears quite quickly. Furthermore, the implied volatility of all of your trades is going to much higher than it would have been otherwise due to the time frame you are dealing with. Near term, options are always going to be more open to large price swings as well.

Buying weekly: Because you are always going to have much less time when it comes to turning a profit with a weekly option, your timing for when to move on a specific decision is going to need to be much more precise than it would otherwise have to be. If you choose poorly at either strike selection, time frame or price direction then you can easily find yourself paying for an option that is generally worthless. You will also need to take into account your level of acceptable risk as the option is going to be cheaper per unit, but you are going to need to purchase more in a week's time than you otherwise would.

Also, it is important to avoid making naked calls or puts when trading on a weekly basis as these typically work out to be lower probability trades as a whole. If you have a bias when it comes to the direction you want your trades to move in, then using a debit spread or structured trade is generally preferred.

Selling weekly: Selling reliably for the long-term can generate steady profits if done properly. It only works this way if you are defining your profits up front, which means it is important to always know what your options are worth to prevent you from selling yourself short. Selling trades weekly will make it easier to collect the full premium if they guess correctly while still leaving you exposed to unmitigated losses if you choose poorly which requires an extra margin.

The ideal types of underlying stock to use for these types of trades is going to be lower priced as they each ultimately consume a smaller amount of your total buying power. This also means it is easier to move forward on trades with lots of implied volatility as it is more likely to revert to the mean in the allotted time. As a rule, selling a put in the short-term is always better than selling a call as it tends to generate an overall higher return in the shorter period.

Spreads: Spreads are a great way of making a profit in the weekly market. The overall level of implied volatility is going to be much higher in the weekly market than in the monthly variation so the spread can help you when you find yourself dealing with an unexpected directional change quickly enough that you can actually do something about it. Selling an option against a long option will naturally decrease the role volatility plays in the transaction. The best point to use the debt spread will be near where the price currently is, providing you with a 1 to 1 risk and reward ratio.

Intraday Trades

While options are frequently left out of day trading strategies, this trend is slowly changing. Traders are slowly but surely realizing that they can apply many standard day trading techniques when it comes to selling and buying options successfully.

Intraday trading challenges: When attempting to day trade options, you are likely going to run into some unique challenges, that you should be able to best with the proper consideration.

1. Price movement will decrease value more significantly due to the time value naturally associated with options that are only near the money so close to their period of expiration. Remember, while their inherent value is likely to increase along with the underlying stock price, which will be dramatically countered by the time value loss.

2. The bid-ask spreads are typically going to be wider than they would otherwise be which is due to the reduced liquidity that you will typically find with the options market. This will frequently vary by as much as .5 of a point which can cut into profits if things move at an inopportune time.

Some types of options are naturally a better fit when it comes to day trading than others. Perhaps the most effective is the near month in the money option which is appropriate for those traders who are a fan of trading stocks with a high level of liquidity. The premium on this type of option is based more closely on its overall value as it is already in the money and getting close to its expiration date. If this occurs, the time value drain is decreased dramatically. This type of option is generally traded most effectively in periods of high volume which tends to result in a decrease in the gap between asking price and bidding price.

Protective put: The protective put is a type of option that is useful when you purchase put orders along with shares of the related underlying stock. This is a reliable strategy when the underlying stock is likely to experience a high degree of volatility. It is especially effective when used to purchase the same option throughout the day to continue to capitalize on short bursts of positive movement. It is also useful when it comes to providing insurance when purchasing shares of a risky underlying stock as you will always be limited in your potential losses to the price of the options you purchased.

Protective puts are also useful in a strategy known as bottom fishing. It is common for many underlying stocks to regularly break through existing support levels and continue moving down into an entirely new lower trading range. When this occurs, it is in your best interest to seek out the bottom point of the downturn so that you can catch it before it starts moving back up. This is easier said than done, however, as it is possible for a stock to give off false signs of having hit bottom and buying in at that point will only lead to serious losses. This is where the protective put comes in, however, and limits the possibility for risk substantially.

While there are models that can be used to calculate the likelihood of the bottom of a given trend, they too can be fooled by the exhausted behavior, which can indicate a false bottom. As such, when you feel that a given stock has bottomed out, then you can buy in with a protective put and then be protected regardless of the ultimate outcome.

Directional options trading: The most effective directional strategies when it comes to intraday options trading are those which have the overall highest degree of making it possible to make quickly moves time and again. These moves are typically going to occur at specific retracement levels or around breakouts.

- Trades that are based around the Fibonacci retracement on the charts for time frames less than 10 minutes. Fibonacci retracements can be used to determine reasonable reward/risk levels either by selling a credit spread to the level in question or through buying options that are already in the money that are likely to experience a bounce at these levels. It is generally going to be in your best interest to look for Fibonacci levels that are likely to overlap at multiple time frames as well as corresponding to the most recent trend experienced by the underlying stock. If you are so inclined, you can also utilize candlestick price patterns as a means of confirming a buy at specific Fibonacci levels.

- Alternately, you may find success with oversold or overbought indicators when it comes to range-bound or trendless stocks. You can then sell credit spreads or buy into options that are already in the money and near the current level of resistance and support with tight stops. It is important to keep in mind that a given stock might not move quickly enough to make these levels worthwhile, so it is important to do your research ahead of time to have a reasonable expectation about the future movement.

- Indicators that are used to signal lower than average volatility such as Bollinger bands are especially useful when it comes to place trades that you anticipate big moves from. Breakout indicators time, especially for the shorter charts, are also especially useful.

High volatility options intraday strategy: Trading volatility by selling options with high volatility, such as credit spreads that are currently out of the money will allow you to make a profit when anticipating a volatility drop. This is a commonly used professional strategy to employ when it comes to earning season or other scenarios where the underlying stock has developed a big price gap. The front month short-term options will then have an extra-large amount of volatility that makes it easier to generate a positive reward and risk ratio when selling. The most common way to take advantage of this fact is through utilizing an iron condor with strike prices of the earning move that is expected to be forthcoming.

Then, before the earnings numbers are announced, you then look up the premiums of at the money calls and get an early idea of what the major players are expecting when it comes to the earnings. This will allow you to determine where you are going to want to place your put credit spread at along with your call credit spread as well. If the stop gap ends up either too low or too high from the expected range, then you still get to keep the premiums. This strategy essentially allows you to trade the way a market maker would through the use of probabilities.

Chapter 12. Volatility in the Markets

While the stock market has long term trends that investors rely on fairly well as the years and decades go by, over the short term the stock market is highly volatile. By that, we mean that prices are fluctuating up and down and doing so over short time periods. Volatility is something that long-term investors ignore. It's why you will hear people that promote conservative investment strategies suggesting that buyers use dollar cost averaging. What this does is it averages out the volatility in the market. That way you don't risk making the mistake of buying stocks when the price is a bit higher than it should be, because you'll average that out by buying shares when it's a bit lower than it should be.

In a sense, over the short term, the stock market can be considered as a chaotic system. So from one day to the next, unless there is something specific on offer, like Apple introducing a new gadget that investors are going to think will be a major hit, you can't be sure what the stock price is going to be tomorrow or the day after that. An increase on one day doesn't mean more increases are coming; it might be followed by a major dip the following day.

For example, at the time of writing, checking Apple's stock price, on the previous Friday it bottomed out at $196. Over the following days, it went up and down several times, and on the most recent close, it was $203. The movements over a short-term period appear random, and to a certain extent, they are. It's only over the long term that we see the actual direction that Apple is heading.

Of course, Apple is at the end of a ten-year run that began with the introduction of the iPhone and iPad. It's a reasonable bet that while it's a solid long-term investment, the stock probably isn't going to be moving enough for the purposes of making good profits over the short term from trades on call options (not too mention the per share price is relatively high).

The truth is volatility is actually a friend of the trader who buys call options. But it's a friend you have to be wary of because you can benefit from volatility while also getting in big trouble from it.

The reason stocks with more volatility are the friend of the options trader is that in part the options trader is playing a probability game. In other words, you're looking for stocks that have a chance of beating the strike price you need in order to make profits. A volatile stock that has large movements has a greater probability of not only passing your strike price but doing so in such a fashion that it far exceeds your strike price enabling you to make a large profit.

Of course, the alternative problem exists – that the stock price will suddenly drop. That is why care needs to be a part of your trader's toolkit. A stock with a high level of volatility is just as likely to suddenly drop in price as it is to skip right past your strike price.

Moreover, while you're a beginner and might get caught with your pants down, volatile stocks are going to attract experienced options traders. That means that the stock will be in high demand when it comes to options contracts. What happens when there is a high demand for something? The price shoots up. In the case of call options, that means the stock will come with a higher premium. You will need to take the higher premium into account when being able to exercise your options at the right time and make sure the price is high enough above your strike price that you don't end up losing money.

Traders take some time to examine the volatility of a given stock over the recent past, but they also look into what's known as implied volatility. This is a kind of weather forecast for stocks. It's an estimate of the future price movements of a stock, and it has a large influence on the pricing of options. Implied volatility is denoted by the Greek symbol σ, implied volatility increases in bear markets, and it actually decreases when investors are bullish. Implied volatility is a tool that can provide insight into the options future value.

For options traders, more volatility is a good thing. A stock that doesn't have much volatility is going to be a stable stock whose price isn't going to change very much over the lifetime of a contract. So while you may want to sell a covered call for a stock with low volatility, you're probably not going to want to buy one if you're buying call options because that means there will be a lower probability that the stock will change enough to exceed the strike price so you can earn a profit on a trade. Remember too that stocks that are very volatile will attract a lot of interest from options traders and command higher premiums. You will have to do some balancing in picking stocks that are of interest.

Being able to pick stocks that will have the right amount of volatility so that you can be sure of getting one that will earn profits on short term trades is something you're only going to get from experience. You should spend some time practicing before actually investing large amounts of money. That is, pick stocks you are interested in and make your bets but don't actually make the trades. Then follow them over the time period of the contract and see what happens. In the meantime, you can purchase safer call options, and so using this two-pronged approach gain experience that will lead to more surefire success down the road.

One thing that volatility means for everyone is that predicting the future is an impossible exercise. You're going to have some misses no matter how much knowledge and experience you gain. The only thing to aim for is to beat the market more often than you lose. The biggest mistake you can make is putting your life savings into a single stock that you think is a sure thing and then losing it all.

Options to pursue if your options aren't working

At this point, you may think that if the underlying stock for your option doesn't go anywhere or it tanks that you have no choice but to wait out the expiration date and count the money you spend on your premiums as a loss. That really isn't the case. The truth is, you can sell a call option you've purchased to other traders in the event its not working for you. Of course, you're not going to make a profit taking this approach in the vast majority of cases. But it will give you a chance to recoup some of your losses. If you have invested in a large number of call options for a specific stock and it's causing you problems, you need to recoup at least some of your losses may be more acute. Of course, the right course of action in these cases is rarely certain, especially if the expiration date for the contract is relatively far off in the future, which could mean that the stock has many chances to turn around and beat your strike price. Remember, in all bad scenarios actually buying the shares of stock is an option – you're not required to do it. In all cases, the biggest loss you're facing is losing the entire premium. You'll also want to keep the following rule of thumb in mind at all times – the more time value an option has, the higher the price you can sell the option for. If there isn't much time value left, then you're probably going to have to sell the option at a discount. If there is a lot of time value, you may be able to recoup most of your losses on the premium.

Let's look at some specific scenarios.

- The stock is languishing. If the stock is losing time value (that is getting closer to the expiration date) and doesn't seem to be going anywhere, you can consider selling the call option in order to recoup some of your losses related to the premium. The more time value, the less likely it is that selling the option is a good idea. Of course, the less time value, the harder it's going to be to actually sell your option. Or put another way, in order to actually sell it you're going to have to take a lower price.

- Suppose the stock isn't stagnant, but it's tanking. If there is a lot of time value left and there is some reason to believe that the company is going to make moves before the expiration date of your contract that will improve the fortunes of the stock when you can still profit from it, then you may want to ride out the downturn. This is a risky judgment call, and it's going to be impossible to know for sure what the right answer is, but you can make an educated guess. On the other hand, if the stock is tanking and there is no good news about the company on the horizon, you are pretty much facing the certainty that you're not going to be able to exercise your options to buy the shares. In that case, you should probably look at selling the option contract to someone more willing to take the risk. At least you can get some of the money back that you paid for the premium.

Now let's briefly consider the positive scenario. Buying options and then trading the stocks can feel like a roller coaster ride, and that rush is what attracts a lot of people to options trading besides the possibilities of making short term profits. Let's consider an example where the stock keeps rising in price? How long do you wait before selling?

There are two risks here. The first risk is that you're too anxious to sell and so do it at the first opportunity. That really isn't a huge downside; you're going to make some profits in that case. On the other hand, it's going to be disconcerting when you sit back and watch the stock continuing to rise. That said, this is better than some of the alternatives.

One of the alternatives is waiting too long to buy and sell the shares. You might wait and see the stock apparently reaching a peak, and then get a little greedy hoping that it's going to keep increasing so you can make even more profits. But then you keep waiting, and suddenly the stock starts dropping. Maybe you wait a little more hoping it's going to start rebounding and going up again, but it doesn't, and you're forced to buy and sell at a lower price than you could have gotten. Maybe it's even dropping enough so that you lose your opportunity altogether. A really volatile stock might suddenly crash, leaving you with a lost opportunity.

The reality is that like everything else involved in options trading since none of us can see the future it's going to be flat out impossible to know if you are making the right call every single time. Keep in mind that your goal is to make a profit on your trades. Don't get greedy about it, hoping for more riches than you actually see on the screen. In other words, the goal isn't to sell at maximum possible profits. Nobody knows what those are because it's going to be virtually impossible to predict what price the stock will peak at before the contract expires. Instead, you're going to want to focus on making an acceptable profit. Before you even buy your call options, you should sit down and figure out a reasonable range of values that define ahead of time what that acceptable profit level is. Then when the stock price hits your target range, you exercise your options and sell the shares. You take your profit and move on, going to the next trades.

That is not a guarantee that you're going to make money on every trade, but it's a more rules-based system that gets you into the mindset of trading based on objective facts rather than relying on unbridled emotions.

Also, remember that you can exercise the option to buy the shares, and then hold them until you think you've reached the right moment to sell. At other times, you may want to exercise the option to buy shares and hold in your portfolio as a long-term investment.

Chapter 13. The Best Strategies to Make Money

Good strategies of any kind of options trading are the major key to any kind of success that is about to be unfolded in any activity. Strategies are normally laid in the trading plan and should be strictly implemented in every options trading move that is likely to be involved. Let us wholly venture into the best strategies so far in options trading.

1.   Collars. The collar strategy is established by holding a number of shares of the underlying stock available in the market where protective puts are bought and the call options sold. In this kind of strategy, the options trader is likely to really protect his or her capital used in the trading activities rather than the idea of acquiring more money during trading. This kind is considered conservative and rather much more important in options trading.

2.   Credit spreads. It is presumed that the biggest fear of most traders is a financial breakdown. In this side of strategy, the trader gets to sell one put and then buy another one.

3.   Covered calls. Covered calls are a good kind of strategy where a particular trader sells the right for another trader to purchase his or her stock at some strike price and get to gain a

good amount of cash. However, there is a specific time that this strategy should be utilized and in a case where the buyer fails to purchase some of the stock and the expiration date dawns, the contract becomes invalid right away.

4.   Cash naked put. Cash naked put is a kind of strategy where the options trader gets to write at the money or out of the money during a particular trading activity and aligning some particular amount of money aside for the purpose of purchasing stock.

5.   Long call strategy. This is the most basic strategy in options trading and the one that is quite easy to comprehend. In the long call strategy for options trading, aggressive option traders who happen to be bullish are pretty much involved. This implies that bullish options traders end up buying stock during the trading activities with the hope of it rising in the near future. The reward is unlimited in the long call strategy.

6.   Short call option strategy. The short call strategy is the reverse of the long call one. Bearish kind of traders is so aggressive in the falling out of stock prices during trading in this kind of strategy. They decide to sell the call options available. This move is considered to be so risky by the experienced options traders believing that prices may drastically decide to rise once again. This significantly implies that large chunks of losses are likely to be incurred, leading to a

real downfall of your trading structure and everything involved in it.

7.   Long put option strategy. First things first, you should be contented that buying a put is the opposite of buying a call. So in this kind of strategy, when you become bearish, that is the moment you may purchase a put option. Put option puts the trader in a situation where he can sell his stock at a particular period of time before the expiration date is reached. This strategy exposes the trader to a mere kind of risk in the options trading market.

8.   Trading time. It is depicted that options trading for a longer period is much value as compared to a short period dating. The longer the trading day, the more skills and knowledge the trader is likely to be engaged into as he or she is likely to get the adequate experience that is needed for good trading. Mastering good trading moves for a while gives the trader the experience and adequate skills.

9.   Bull call spread strategy. In this kind of strategy, the investor gets to purchase several calls at a particular strike price and then purchases the price at a much higher price. The calls always bear a similar expiration date and come from the same underlying stock. This type of strategy is mostly implemented by the bullish options traders.

10.   Bear put strategy. This strategy involves a trader purchasing put options at a particular price amount and later selling off at a lower price amount. These options bear a similar expiration date and from the same underlying stock. This strategy is mostly utilized by traders who are said to be bearish. The consequences are limited losses and limited gains.

11.   Iron condor. The iron condor involves the bull call spread strategy and the bear put strategy all at the same time during a particular trading period. The expiration dates of the stock are still similar and are of the same underlying stock. Most traders get to use this strategy when the market is expected to experience low volatility rates and with the expectation of gaining a little amount of premium. Iron condor works in both up and down markets are is really believed to be economical during the up and down markets.

12.   Married put strategy. On this end, the options trader purchase options at a particular amount of money and at the same time, get to buy the same number of shares of the underlying stock. This kind of strategy is also known as the protective put. This is also a bearish kind of options trading strategy.

13.   Cash covered put strategy. Here, one or more contracts are sold with a 100 shares multiplied with the strike price amount for every particular contract involved in the options trading. Most traders use this strategy to acquire an extra

amount of premium on a specific stock they would wish to purchase.

14.   Long or short calendar spread strategy. This is a tricky type of strategy. The market stock is said to be stagnant, not moving and waiting for the right timing until the expiration of the front-month is reached.

15.   Synthetic long arbitrage strategy. Most traders take advantage of this strategy when they are trying to take advantage of the different market prices in different kinds of markets with just the same property.

16.   Put ratio back spread strategy. This is a bearish type of options strategy where the trader gets to sell some put options and gets to purchase more options of just the same underlying stock with a similar expiration date and a lower price.

17.   Call ratio back spread. In this strategy, the trader uses both the long and short options positions so as to eradicate consistent losses and target achieving large loads of benefits over a particular trading period. The essence of this strategy is to generate profits in case the stock prices tend to elevate and reduce the number of risks likely to be involved. This strategy is mostly implemented by bullish kind of options traders.

18.   Long butterfly strategy. This strategy involves three parts where one put option is purchased at particular and then selling

the other two options at a price lower than the buying price and purchasing one put at even lower price during a particular trading period.

19.   Short butterfly strategy. In this strategy, three parts are still involved where a put option is sold at a much higher price and two puts are then purchased at a lower price than the purchase price and a put option is later on sold at a much lower strike price. In both cases, all put bear the same expiration date and the strike prices are normally equidistant as revealed in various options trading charts. A short butterfly strategy is the reverse way of the long butterfly strategy.

20.   Long straddle. The long straddle is also known as the buy strangle where a slight pull and a slight call are purchased during a particular period before the expiration date reaches. The importance of this strategy is that the trader bears a large chance of acquiring good amounts of profits during his or her trading time before the expiration date is achieved.

21.   Short straddle. In this kind of strategy, the trader sells both the call and put options at a similar price and bearing the same expiration date. Traders practice this strategy with the hope of acquiring good amounts of profits and experience limited various kinds of risks.

22.   Owning positions that are already in a portfolio. Most traders prefer purchasing and selling various options that

already hedge existing positions. This kind of strategy method is believed to incur good profits and incur losses too in other occurrences.

23.   Albatross trade strategy. This kind of strategy aims at gaining some amounts of profits when the market is stagnant during a specific options trading period or a pre-determined period of time. This kind of strategy is similar to the short gut strategy.

24.   Reverse iron condor strategy. This kind of strategy focuses on benefiting some profits when the underlying stock in the current market dares to make some sharp market trade moves in either direction. Eventually, a limited amount of risks are experienced and a limited amount of profits during trading.

25.   Iron butterfly spread. Buying and holding four different options in the market at three different market prices is involved in the trading market for a particular trading period.

26.   Short bull ratio strategy. Short bull ratio strategy is used to benefit from the amounts of profits gained from increasing security involved in the trading market in a similar way in which we normally get to buy calls during a particular period.

27.   Bull condor spread. This is a type of strategy that is designed to return a profit if the actual price of security decides to rise to a predicted price range during a specific trading

period impacting good chunks of profits made to the options trader and a limited number of risks involved.

28. Put ratio spread strategy. This strategy entails purchasing a number of put options and adding more options with various strike prices and equal kind of underlying stock during a particular options trading period.

29. Strap straddle strategy. Strap straddle strategy uses one put and two calls bearing a similar strike price and with an equal date of expiration and also containing the same underlying stock that is normally stagnant during a particular trading period. The trader utilizes this type of strategy for the hope of getting higher amounts of profits as compared to the regular straddle strategy over a particular period of the trading period.

30. Strap strangle strategy. This strategy is bullish, where more call options are purchased as compared to the put options and a bullish inclination is then depicted in various trading charts information.

31. Put back spread strategy. This back spread strategy combines both the short puts and long puts so as to establish a position where the ratio of losses and profits entirely depends on the ratio of their two puts that are likely to be experienced in the market.

32. Short call ratio. This strategy involves purchasing a single call and later on selling two other calls at a higher price amount during a specific period of time before its expiration. This concept combines the protocols of the bull call spread strategy and the naked call strategy. The essence of this strategy is to acquire limited loss potential and mixed profits potential to the options trader involved during a particular period of time.

33. Iron albatross strategy. The particular trader gets to use this type of strategy when expecting a particular underlying stock to trade during a particular period of time before expiration. Four transactions are usually involved in this strategy and a high level of trading is called for. This implies that this measure kind is so suitable for the experienced traders, ones who have mastered almost every market move.

34. Bull call ladder spread strategy. This one is almost similar to the bull call strategy where security increasing in price is expected to source out some profits to the trader during options trading.

Chapter 14. Top Trader Mistakes to Avoid in Options Trading

Options trading is an entirely different animal as compared to normal stock market investing. Let's think for a moment about the common wisdom that is dispensed with regard to stock market investing. The general idea is to buy and hold, keeping your investments for a very long period of time. In fact, basically, you're expected to keep your investments until retirement. People do various strategies such as rebalancing their portfolio to match their goals, diversification, and dollar-cost averaging.

Options trading is a totally different way of looking at things. First of all, even if you are a day trader or engaging in activities like swing trading, the general goal, when it comes to stocks, is to buy when the price is at a relatively low point, and then sell at a high price. In reality, the day trader, the swing trader, and the buy-and-hold investor are no different. Buy-and-hold investors think that they are special and above everyone else, they are in reality just trying to make money off the stock market too. The only real difference, unless you are a dividend investor, is the time frame involved. So your buy-and-hold investor is going to hold the stocks for 25 years, and then they are going to start cashing them out for money. A swing trader makes money in the here and now.

So in that sense of options trading is more like swing trading. And in fact, in many cases, you're looking for the same price swings that the swing trader seeks. But as we've seen, options allow many strategies that are not available for any type of stock market investor. I suppose that in theory, you could buy huge numbers of shares of stock and try to set up similar arrangements, but it just wouldn't work. And besides that, even if it did it would require an enormous amount of capital.

The point of this discussion is to just lay out the groundwork and acknowledged that most of us come to options with a completely different mindset. So does take some getting used to and many beginning options traders are going to make mistakes. That's just the nature of the market because it's so different than what people are used to.

In this chapter, we are going to review some of the top mistakes are made by beginning options traders. There isn't really a comprehensive list, I picked out the ones that I've noticed most people make the mistake of doing.

Going into a Trade Too Big

One of the mistakes that people make when they start out options trading is making their positions too big. Since our options don't cost all that much relative to the price for stocks, people aren't used to trading in small amounts. Even people who are not rich or anything thinking terms of the stock price and how much 100 shares with the cost. This can set up people for trouble. The temptation is going to be there to move on a large number of contracts when you start doing your trades, if you have the capital to purchase or sell them. This can actually get people into trouble. It's not really the dollar amount that's a concern, but it could get you in a position where you're not really ready to act as quickly as you might need to depend on the situation. So if you find trade and decide to sell 20 contracts, in the event that the trade goes south trying to buyback does 20 contracts might be problematic. Or you might end up buying a bunch of call options and have trouble getting out of them on the same day. It's actually better to have a few different small positions with the options than it is to have multiple positions when they are a large number. Remember that options prices move fast. You don't want to over-leverage your trades and be in a position where you can't find a buyer to pick up all 10 or 20 contracts.

Not Paying Attention to Expiration

This is probably one of the most common mistakes made by beginning traders. The expiration date is one of the most important factors that should be considered as you enter your trades. And once you've entered a trade, you need to have the expiration date of the options tattooed on your forehead. This is something that is not amenable to being ignored. First of all, choosing the expiration date when entering the position is just as important as picking the strike price of the option. But one of the things that beginners do is to focus too much on the price of the option and the price-setting for the strike. The cost of the option and the strike price are obviously very important, the expiration date is important as well.

Unfortunately, far too many beginning traders ignore the expiration date when their trades are not working out. And so, they end up just letting the option expires. Of course, when that happens if it's out of the money, you are totally out of luck. It's just going to be at 100% loss. So, we need to be paying attention to expiration dates before we actually enter the trade, and we also need to pay attention expiration dates when we are managing the trade.

Buying Cheap Options

There is a saying that says you get what you pay for. There are reasons to buy out of the money options sometimes, but you shouldn't go too far out of the money. Unfortunately, many beginning traders are tempted to go far out of the money for the sake of buying a low-priced option. The problem with these options is that even though out of the money options can make profits. If they're too far out of the money, they simply aren't going to see any action. So, there's no sense buying a cheap option just because you can pick it up for $25. You don't want to be sinking your money into options where a massive price move would be necessary in order to earn any profits. It's fine to buy options that are near at the money. Options that are close to being in the money can be very profitable even though they are out of the money. So, if you're looking to save a little bit of money when starting out your investing, that is always something to consider. But to make profits, the basic rule is there has to be some reasonable chance that's the stock prices going to move enough, in order to make the option you purchase going the money.

Failing to Close when Selling Options

If you want to remember just one thing from our discussion about selling options, whether it's selling put credit spreads or naked puts, you should keep in mind that it's always possible to exit the trade. The way that you exit the trade when you sell to open is you buy to close. You want to be careful about doing this because it's too easy to give in to your emotions and panic and prematurely exit a trade. However, you need to be aware at all times of the possibility of needing to close the trade. Riding out an option all the way to expiration is a foolish move unless it's very clear that it's going to expire out of the money.

As a part of this problem, new options traders often come to the market and they focus on hope as a strategy. When it comes to investing, hope is definitely not a strategy. Hope is something that belongs to a casino playing slot machine games. When you're training options, you should make as rational a decision as you can make it given the circumstances. So when the expiration date is closing and it's clear that the trade is not going to be profitable, don't give in to the temptation to say of waiting around for a reversal in direction. When you say something like that to yourself, that opens up the temptation to stay in the trade far too long. At some point, you might not be able to recover at all. So what you don't want to do, and this is true buying and selling, is hoping that there's going to be a turnaround and waiting to see what happens.

For those who are buying options to open their positions, this is the worst of all possible strategies. Remember that when you buy to open a position, time decay is working against you at all times. So unless the stock is moving in a good direction, there isn't a reason to hold the option. For sellers, time decay actually works in your favor. But there can be situations when it's just smart to get out of the trade. Let's look at a couple of examples.

If you sell to open an iron condor, and for some reason, the stock has a breakout to one direction or the other, it's better to get out of the iron Condor now. We aren't talking about a one or two dollar change. If the stock goes in such a direction that one of your options goes in the money by a small amount, that type of trade is worth waiting out to see what happens. But if there is a big break to the upside or the downside, it would be foolish to stay in the trade. For one thing, there would be at risk of assignment, but the most likely situation is that you're just going to lose the maximum amount of money. But if you have a good strategy and only getting involved with options that have a high level of open interest, almost no matter what the situation is, you should be able to buy and sell that option pretty quickly.

The other obvious example is if you were selling a put credit spread already naked put, and you noticed that the share price is declining right towards your strike price. You don't have to panic right away because remember that in order for exercising the option to be worthwhile, the share price has to move enough, so that not only does the option go in the money, but the price move also accounts for the money that was paid for the premium to buy the contract. So, if you have a strike price of $100 and someone paid two dollars to buy the option, if the share price is $99, they are going to exercise the option. Even if it drops to $98, they still might not exercise the option, unless there was some factor to indicate that the stock was about to turn around so they can sell it at a profit. But that's an unlikely scenario. It's only when it starts going strong and that there's a problem.

Trading Illiquid Options

This is such an important issue I will say it again. Liquidity is very important when trading options. What liquidity means is the ability to buy and sell financial security quickly, and turn it into cash. It's not enough to like the company in order to start trading options on the company. If the open interest for an option is only 8, 10, or even 45, that is going to throw up obstacles when you need to move to get rid of an option fast. The largest companies generally have liquid options, but you should always check. Index funds also have liquid options. Avoid any companies that have small open interests. The only way that you would trade when the open interest with small is if the probability of losing out on the trade is minuscule. So besides the strike price, share price, an expiration date, you need to be looking closely at open interest. You don't want to get in a situation where you cannot exit a position.

Not Having a Trading Plan

One of the best things about options trading is that it's very easy. So, you have this relatively low-cost way to get involved in the stock market, and it's also relatively easy to manage on your own. These are positives generally speaking, but there is a downside. That downside is the fact that it's so easy people just start trading on a whim. Make no mistake, just because it's easy, that doesn't mean the money and potential losses are not real. So you need to treat this with the utmost seriousness. Take some time to develop a trading plan. The trading plan should include many of the things we mentioned earlier, such as the level of profit that you're willing to accept on any trade. It should also set up a limit that is used to determine when to exit your positions. But I forgot to mention one thing that is really important. Your trading plan should also pick out a maximum of five financial securities that you are going to focus on when trading options. In my opinion, doing more than five financial securities is more than your mind can handle. The reason I say that, is that you should be keeping close watching over each of the companies for index funds that you were trading. If you have more than five, that isn't really going to be possible. And as I've said before, one of the things about options trading is that the pricing can move very quickly. So if you're trying to spread your attention in 20 different directions, you're probably going to end up losing money because you simply aren't able to keep track of everything.

You should also include some diversity in your trading plan. When you pick out the five securities that you are going to use for the next year to trade your options, don't pick them all from the same sector. You can pick a couple from the same sector, but be sure to have a couple that is different. I also actually recommend trading one or two index funds. Some of the index funds that are available, in particular, SPY and QQQ, are great for options trading because they are super liquid. There is only one danger that you have to worry about with index funds. And that is that there is a certain sensitivity of the major market indices to news and political events. The problem with that is political and news events tend to be pretty random. So that it can make it hard sometimes to enter a position like a puts credit spread, when you just never know what the next tweet is going to be. However, generally speaking, index funds are great to include the financial securities that you're willing to trade options on.

Failing to have an exit plan

As I mentioned earlier in the book, you should have an exit plan for every one of your trades. I prefer to have an overall exit plan and have every trade follow the same basic rules. An exit plan will help you minimize your losses. This goes back to the problem of beginning traders holding onto an option until the expiration date. That is more likely to happen if you haven't formulated a strategy to exit your position. You can be helpful to keep a notebook to record all your trades and write down the rules for each trade. That way you can refer to it when things are fluctuating about, and possibly putting you into a situation where there are catastrophic losses. Now, of course, they aren't really catastrophic, assuming that you are reasonable in the number of options contracts that you trade in a single move. But you want to have some kind of rule so that you will exit the trade if the losses exceed a certain amount. Of course, sometimes, you're going to make a mistake. So, in other words, if you have some kind of rules such as you are going to sell to close if the loss reaches $50, something I can guarantee is at some point, you are going to do that but the stock is going to rebound and if you had stayed in, you would've made $200 or something like that. You just have to accept that, sometimes, if you are going to miss out on situations like that. But on average, that's not really likely to happen. So, if an option is going south and you have a $50 exit rule, it's a good idea to just follow it and live with the consequences.

A similar situation happens on the other side. So as I suggested, I maintain a $50 profit rule. So, whenever I've invested in options and it reaches $50 dollars per contract profit, I exit the trade. There are going to be times when the profit could've been $100 or even $200. So, when you have a rule like that you are going to miss out on some upside once in a while. But most of the time, what happens is traders stay in the trade too long. And then they end up losing money, so maybe you are losing $25 instead of having been a little bit conservative and making a $50 profit. The level of profit that you choose is entirely up to you. But the point is you should have some fixed value and always follow that rule the matter what.

Chapter 15. Risk Management

Excellent risk management can save the worst trading strategy, but horrible risk management will sink even the best strategy. This is a lesson that many traders learn painfully over time, and I suggest you learn this by heart and install it deep within you even if you can't fully comprehend that statement.

Risk management has many different elements to both quantitative and qualitative. When it comes to options trading, the quantitative side is minimal thanks to the nature of options limiting risk by themselves. However, the qualitative side deserves a lot of attention. This chapter is going to give you the risk management framework that you need to succeed.

Risk

So what is risk anyway? Logically, it is the probability of you losing all of your money. In trading terms, you can think of it as being the probability of your actions putting you on a path to losing all of your capital. A good way to think about the need for good risk management is to ask yourself what a bad trader would do? Forget trading, what would a bad business person do with their capital?

Well, they would spend it on useless stuff that adds nothing to the bottom line. They would also increase expenses, market poorly, not take care of their employees, and be indiscipline with regards to their processes. While trading, you don't have employees or marketing needs, so you don't need to worry about that.

Do you have suppliers and costs? Well, yes, you do. Your supplier is your broker, and you pay fees to execute your trades. That is the cost of access. In directional trading, you have high costs as well because taking losses is a necessary part of trading. With market neutral or non-directional trading, your losses are going to be minimal, but you should still seek to minimize them.

What about discipline? Do you think you can trade and analyze the market well if you've just returned home from your job and are tired? If you didn't sleep properly last night? Or if you've argued with your spouse or partner? The point I'm making is that the more you behave like a terrible business owner, the more you increase your risk of failure.

Odds and Averages

Trading requires you to think a bit differently about profitability. In the previous paragraphs, I spoke about minimizing costs, and your first thought must have been to seek to reduce losses and maximize wins. This is a natural product of linear or ordered thinking. The market, however, is chaotic and linear thinking is going to get you nowhere.

Instead, you need to think in terms of averages and odds. Averages imply that you need to worry about your average loss size and your average win size. Seek to decrease the former and increase the latter. Notice that when we talk about averages, we're not necessarily talking about reducing the total number of losses. You can reduce the average by either reducing the sum of your losses or by increasing the number of losing trades while keeping the sum of the losses constant. This is a shift in thinking you must make.

Thinking in this way sets you up nicely to think in terms of odds, because in chaotic systems all you can bank on are odds playing out in the long run. For example, if you flip a coin, do you know in advance whether it's going to be a heads or tails? Probably not. But if someone asked you to predict the distribution of heads versus tails over 10,000 flips, you could reasonably guess that it'll be 5000 heads and 5000 tails. You might be off by a few flips either way, but you'll be pretty close percentage-wise.

In fact, the greater the number of flips, the lesser your error percentage. This is because the odds inherent in a pattern that occurs in a chaotic system express themselves best over the long run. Your trading strategy is precisely such a pattern. The market is a chaotic system. Hence, you should focus on executing your strategy as it is meant to be executed over and over again and worry about profitability only in the long run.

Contrast this with the usual attitude of traders who seek to win every single trade. This is impossible to accomplish since no trading strategy or pattern is correct 100% of the time. If we were discussing directional strategies, I'd spend a lot more time on this, but the fact is that options take care of a lot of this ambiguity themselves.

This is because you don't have to do much when trading options. You enter and then monitor the trade. Sure, it helps to have some directional bias, but even if you get it wrong, your losses will be extremely limited, and you're more likely to hit winners than losers.

Despite this, always think of your strategy in terms of its odds. There are two basic metrics to measure this. The first is the win rate of your system. This is simply the percentage of winners you have. The second is your payout ratio which is the average win size divided by the average loss size.

Together these two metrics will determine how profitable your system is. Both of them play off one another, and an increase in one is usually met by a decrease in another. It takes an extremely skillful trader to increase both simultaneously.

Risk Per Trade

The quantitative side of risk management when it comes to options trading is lesser than what you need to take care of when trading directionally. However, this doesn't mean there's nothing to worry about. Perhaps the most important metric of them all is your risk per trade. The risk per trade is what ultimately governs your profitability.

How much should you risk per trade? Common wisdom says that you should restrict this to 2% of your capital. For options trading purposes, this is perfectly fine. In fact, once you build your skill and can see opportunities better, I'd suggest increasing it to a higher level.

A point that you must understand here is that you must keep your risk per trade consistent for it to have any effect. You might see a wonderful setup and think that it has no chance of failure, but the truth is that you don't know how things will turn out. Even the prettiest setup has every chance of failing, and the ugliest setup you can think of may result in a profit. So never adjust your position size based on how something looks.

Calculating your position size for a trade is a pretty straightforward task. Every option's strategy will have a fixed maximum risk amount. Divide the capital risk by this amount, and that gives you your position size. Round that down to the nearest whole number since you can only buy whole number lots when it comes to contract sizes.

For example, let's say your maximum risk is $50 per lot on the trade. Your capital is $10,000. Your risk per trade is 2%. So the amount you're risking on that trade is 2% of 10,000 which is $200. Divide this by 50, and you get 4. Hence, your position size is four contracts or 400 shares. (You'll buy the contracts, not the shares.)

Why is it important to keep your risk per trade consistent? Well, recall that your average win and loss size is important when it comes to determining your profitability. These, in conjunction with your strategy's success rate, determine how much money you'll make. If you keep shifting your risk amount per trade, you'll shift your win and loss sizes. You might argue that since it's an average, you can always adjust amounts to reflect an average.

My counter to that is how would you know which trades to adjust in advance? You won't know which ones are going to be a win or a loss, so you won't know which trade sizes to adjust to meet the average. Hence, keep it consistent across all trades and let the math work for you.

Aside from risk per trade, there are some simple metrics you should keep track of as part of your quantitative risk management plan.

Drawdown

A drawdown refers to the reduction in capital your account experiences. Drawdowns by themselves always occur. The metrics you should be measuring are the maximum drawdown and recovery period. If you think of your account's balance as a curve, the maximum drawdown is the biggest peak to trough distance in dollars. The recovery period is the subsequent time it took for your account to make new equity high.

If your risk per trade is far too high, your max drawdown will be unacceptably high. For example, if you risk 10% per trade and lose two in a row, which is very likely, your drawdown is going to be 20%. This is an absurdly large hole to dig your way out. Consider that your capital has decreased by 20% and the subsequent climb back up needs to be done on lesser capital than previously.

This is why you need to keep your risk per trade low and in line with your strategy's success rate. The best way to manage drawdowns and limit the damage they cause is to put in place risk limits per day, week, and month. Even professional athletes who train to do one thing all the time have bad days, so it's unfair to expect yourself to be at 100% all the time.

These risk limits will take you out of the game when you're playing poorly. A daily risk limit is to prevent you from getting into a spiral of revenge trading. A good limit to stick to when starting off is to stop trading if you experience three losses in a row. This is pretty unlikely with options trades to be honest unless you screw up badly, but it's good to have a limit in place from a perspective of discipline.

Next, aim for a maximum weekly drawdown limit of 5% and a monthly drawdown limit of 6-8%. These are pretty high limits, to be honest, and if you are a directional trader, these limits do not apply to you. Directional traders need to be a lot more conservative than options trader when it comes to risk.

Understand that these are hard stop limits. So if your account has hit its monthly drawdown level within the first week, you need to take the rest of the month off. Overtrading and a lack of reflection on progress can cause a lot of damage, and a drawdown is simply a reflection of that.

Qualitative Risk

Quantitative metrics aside, your ability to properly manage qualitative things in your life and trading will dictate a lot of your success. Prepare well, and you're likely to see progress. You need to see preparation as your responsibility. I mean, no one else can prepare for you can they?

There are different elements to tracking your level of preparation so let's look at them one by one.

Health

You can't trade if you're physically unfit. If you have a fever or if you're suffering from some condition that makes it impossible for you to concentrate, forget about trading. You can rest assured that the other traders in the market will be more than happy to take your money.

When viewed from an options trading perspective, the risk is even more acute. All options strategies will require you to write options at some point, even the most basic ones like in this book. Even if your position is covered, making a mistake, and having an option you wrote be exercised by the buyer is an unpleasant thing that happens. Maintain a regimen of exercise and eat healthy food. Depending on how long you sit in front of your screen, you might even want to consider avoiding certain foods when in session.

Heavy meals and food that makes you drowsy will cause your performance to dip, so avoid eating them when you're in the market. Also, don't exercise to such an extent that you're completely exhausted. The idea is to be fresh and alert, not fatigued and aching for a good sleep.

You might have an image of traders as being highly wired and as people who spend their entire lives in front of a screen. Well, most traders do sit in front of a screen most of the time, but the successful ones make time for other stuff in their lives as well.

So don't try to copy some false vision here. Instead, do what feels comfortable to you while taking care to not slip into habits that are detrimental to your success.

Lifestyle

Your fitness is just one part of your lifestyle, of course. Is your lifestyle conducive to profitable trading? Are you someone who loves staying up at all sorts of odd hours and considers it perfectly normal to stumble onto a work task while hungover or worse? Make no mistake, the market will make you donate all of your capital to it.

Many beginners underestimate how difficult trading is. This should come as no surprise since beginners by definition underestimate anything. What shocks most of them is the degree to which they underestimate the difficulty of trading successfully. Let me put it in writing for you: Trading is one of the most challenging things you will ever do in your life.

The reason it is so difficult is due to the ever-changing nature of the market and the mental demands it places upon you. Another key lifestyle question to consider is the hours when you'll trade. Most of you reading this probably have full-time jobs and cannot spend your whole day in front of the market.

So plan out when you'll trade and how you'll prepare yourself for the session. What routines will you carry out? If you're going to trade in the morning before work begins, how will you manage to do this? Will you work in a quiet place or in some noisy truck stop on the way to work? Options positions don't need a lot of maintenance, so there's not much need for this, but when will you check in on the market throughout the day? Will you check in a few times? Five times? Define everything to do with your routine.

Think of yourself as a professional athlete who has to show up for a game everyday. An athlete has a precise method of preparation before showing up for a game. They don't deviate from their preparatory routine and certainly don't experiment with new things during game time. Practice is when they try out new stuff.

How will you practice your skills and improve your ability to execute your strategy? When will you do this? Plan it all out and develop your success routine.

Mental States

Trading is a mental activity. You don't need to lift or push anything physically. Therefore it is crucial to ensure that your mental state is as optimal as it needs to be for you to execute properly. Having a checklist or a mental check-in list works wonders for the trading process.

Before any trading, write down what's going through your mind and ask yourself how you feel. If you find that you're tired or frustrated and unable to focus properly, step away, and do not trade. If you're planning on sitting in front of your terminal for more than an hour, make it a habit to check in with yourself every half hour or hourly. This need not be a detailed examination, just a simple check-in with yourself to see how things are going.

Take your risk management tasks seriously, and the market will reward you with profits. Do not be the trader who stumbles into the market completely unprepared and then wonders why trading is so unforgiving. Above all else, seek to eliminate all sources of stress when it comes to trading. Take regular breaks and schedule months off from the market to recap and assimilate the things you've learned and need to improve.

Trading every single day of the year does not make sense. This isn't a job where you'll be rewarded with a certain salary for just showing up. You need to produce results, and in order to do so, you need to manage your downside carefully.

An excellent practice is to actually review how you work and set aside months exclusively for trading and months exclusively for practice purposes. By practice, I mean reviewing your prior results, working on your mindset and improving your risk management abilities. This is an unconventional method of working but it will pay massive dividends down the line.

Now that you have a better understanding of the basics, it's finally time to jump in and take a look at various trading strategies you can deploy with options.

Conclusion

Besides understanding the basics of options, the most important thing to learn is the wide range of strategies that can be used when it comes to options. These strategies open a lot of doors for traders to make profits that would not be available otherwise.

When you are learning, you should try out all the strategies to see what works best for you. Everyone is going to have their own tastes, but options trading is so different that you need to try things out before you get stuck only buying call options, which is a mistake that happens to a lot of beginners who are afraid to try the many different strategies that options trading has to offer.

One of my favorite things about options is that you can get involved in options trading without having very much money. If people were smart and disciplined about it, options trading could even provide a way out of a low-income situation. You can start trading with a hundred dollars, and if you are careful with it a year from now, there is no reason that you could not significantly grow that into a large trading account.

Just remember that options trading is a serious business, but it can be fun and exciting too. There is no reason why making money has to be tedious and difficult. You can get involved at the highest levels of our economy with the best companies, by trading options. Hopefully, you will be able to ride the wave on the stock market and earn some of your own profits.

Remember that options trading is flexible, so when the market enters a downturn, don't stop trading! You can keep going and earn profits as the share price goes down and everyone else is panicking.

Thank you again for taking the time to read this book, and if you have enjoyed the book, please leave a review for us on Amazon. We will enjoy hearing from you about your trading experiences!

CPSIA information can be obtained
at www.ICGtesting.com
Printed in the USA
BVHW041418030621
608729BV00004B/1507